UK

Instant Vortex Air Fryer Cookbook

for Beginners

1800 Days of Low-Fat, Low-Carb, Time-Saving Air Fryer Recipes, Air Roast, Baking, Dehydrating, Broiling, Reheating for Busy Families

Homemade Cooking

Alfie Barrett

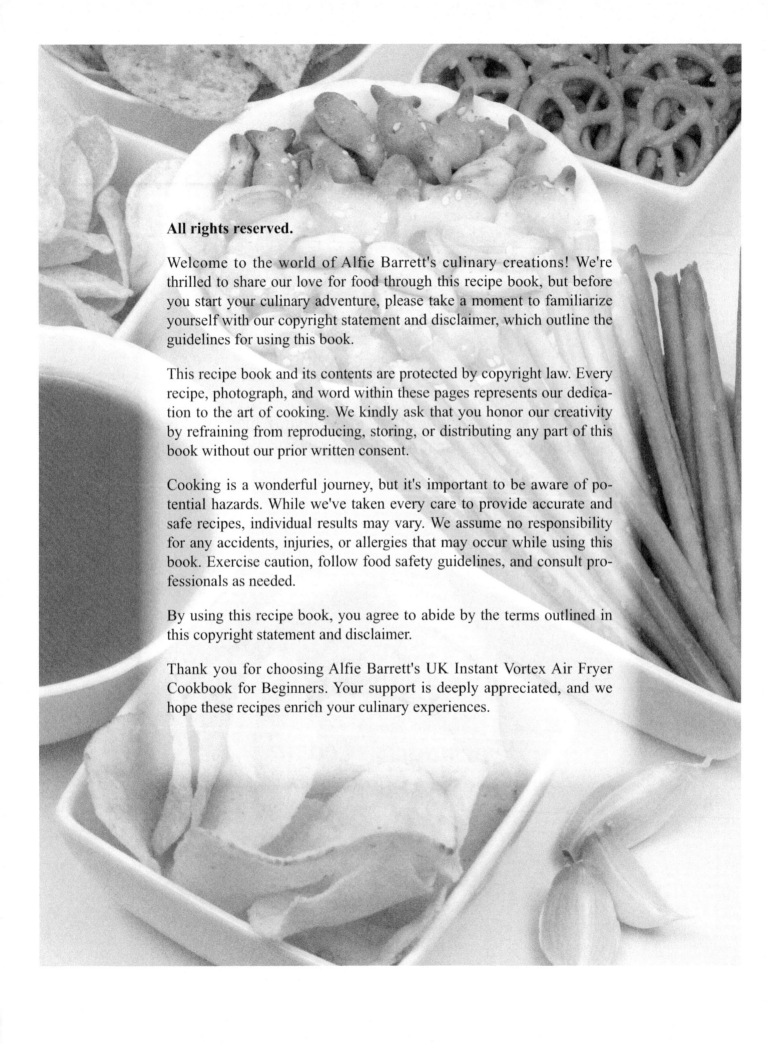

CONTENTS

INTRODUCTION 7

Understanding Air Frying 8
Common Cooking Modes for Air Fryers 8
6 Tips and Tricks for the Instant Vortex Air Fryer 9

Breakfast & Snacks And Fries Recipes 10

Hard Boiled Eggs Air Fryer Style 11
Easy Air Fryer Sausage 11
Swede Fries 11
Wholegrain Pitta Chips 11
Breakfast Eggs & Spinach 12
Courgette Fries 12
Polenta Fries 12
Loaded Hash Browns 13
Potato Fries 13
Oozing Baked Eggs 13
Blueberry & Lemon Breakfast Muffins 13
Morning Sausage Wraps 14
Cumin Shoestring Carrots 14
Easy Cheese & Bacon Toasties 14
Your Favourite Breakfast Bacon 14
Delicious Breakfast Casserole 14
French Toast 15
Monte Cristo Breakfast Sandwich 15
Crunchy Mexican Breakfast Wrap 15
Healthy Stuffed Peppers 16
Mexican Breakfast Burritos 16
Easy Cheesy Scrambled Eggs 16
Avocado Fries 16
Egg & Bacon Breakfast Cups 17
Cheesy Sausage Breakfast Pockets 17
Bocconcini Balls 17
Pitta Pizza 17
Blanket Breakfast Eggs 18
Blueberry Bread 18
Easy Omelette 18
Breakfast Sausage Burgers 18

Sauces & Snack And Appetiser Recipes 19

Spring Rolls 20
Beetroot Crisps 20
Sweet Potato Crisps 20
Snack Style Falafel 20
Garlic Cheese Bread 21
Pao De Queijo 21
Lumpia 21
Jalapeño Poppers 21
Tortellini Bites 22
Popcorn Tofu 22
Mac & Cheese Bites 22
Korean Chicken Wings 22
Air-fried Pickles 23
Onion Bahji 23
Bacon Smokies 23
Salt And Vinegar Chickpeas 23
Mozzarella Sticks 24
Peppers With Aioli Dip 24
Pork Jerky 24
Spicy Peanuts 24
Onion Pakoda 25
Tostones 25
Cheese Wontons 25
Pepperoni Bread 25
Salt And Vinegar Chips 26
Jalapeño Pockets 26

Asian Devilled Eggs 26
Stuffed Mushrooms 26
Pretzel Bites 27

Pasta Chips 27
Thai Bites 27

Vegetarian & Vegan Recipes 28

Roasted Vegetable Pasta...........................29
Potato Gratin 29
Pakoras..29
Courgette Burgers 30
Onion Dumplings 30
Spring Ratatouille 30
Vegan Fried Ravioli 30
Shakshuka 31
Courgette Meatballs 31
Vegan Meatballs 31
Chickpea And Sweetcorn Falafel..............32
Tofu Bowls 32
Roasted Cauliflower 32
Air-fried Artichoke Hearts 33
Tempura Veggies 33
Ratatouille 33

Air Fryer Cheese Sandwich 33
Sweet Potato Taquitos..............................34
Veggie Bakes..34
Baked Feta, Tomato & Garlic Pasta...........34
Spicy Spanish Potatoes 34
Lentil Balls With Zingy Rice 35
Goat's Cheese Tartlets..............................35
Falafel Burgers 35
Artichoke Pasta 36
Radish Hash Browns 36
Miso Mushrooms On Sourdough Toast 36
Whole Wheat Pizza...................................36
Spanakopita Bites.....................................37
Buffalo Cauliflower Bites 37
Jackfruit Taquitos 37

Side Dishes Recipes 38

Sweet Potato Tots.....................................39
Aubergine Parmesan 39
Egg Fried Rice 39
Butternut Squash......................................39
Super Easy Fries 40
Carrot & Parmesan Chips 40
Alternative Stuffed Potatoes 40
Zingy Brussels Sprouts 40
Mediterranean Vegetables 41
Orange Tofu 41
Corn On The Cob 41
Tex Mex Hash Browns...............................41
Mexican Rice 42
Orange Sesame Cauliflower......................42
Cauliflower With Hot Sauce And Blue Cheese Sauce
42

Air Fryer Eggy Bread................................43
Grilled Bacon And Cheese........................43
Potato Hay..43
Zingy Roasted Carrots 43
Potato Wedges With Rosemary.................44
Roasted Okra..44
Sweet And Sticky Parsnips And Carrots....44
Cheesy Garlic Asparagus 44
Air Fryer Corn On The Cob.......................44
Cheesy Broccoli 45
Honey Roasted Parsnips 45
Sweet Potato Wedges...............................45
Garlic And Parsley Potatoes.....................45
Crispy Cinnamon French Toast.................46
Sweet & Spicy Baby Peppers....................46
Ricotta Stuffed Aubergine........................46

Poultry Recipes

Smoky Chicken Breast.................................48
Chicken Tikka Masala.................................48
Sticky Chicken Tikka Drumsticks.................48
Olive Stained Turkey Breast........................49
Chicken & Potatoes....................................49
Chicken And Wheat Stir Fry........................49
Whole Chicken...49
Pizza Chicken Nuggets...............................50
Healthy Bang Bang Chicken........................50
Bacon Wrapped Chicken Thighs..................50
Crispy Cornish Hen....................................51
Buttermilk Chicken.....................................51
Chicken Balls, Greek-style...........................51
Chicken And Cheese Chimichangas.............51
Pepper & Lemon Chicken Wings.................52
Charred Chicken Breasts.............................52

Air Fryer Chicken Thigh Schnitzel................52
Turkey And Mushroom Burgers...................52
Air Fryer Bbq Chicken................................53
Cornflake Chicken Nuggets.........................53
Honey Cajun Chicken Thighs......................53
Buffalo Wings..53
Grain-free Chicken Katsu............................54
Chicken Tikka...54
Chicken Kiev..55
Chicken Jalfrezi..55
Air Fryer Sesame Chicken Thighs................55
Buffalo Chicken Wontons...........................55
Chicken Fried Rice......................................56
Bbq Chicken Tenders..................................56
Chicken Milanese.......................................56

Beef & Lamb And Pork Recipes

Hamburgers...58
Traditional Empanadas...............................58
Breaded Pork Chops...................................58
Asparagus & Steak Parcels.........................58
Italian Meatballs..59
Cheesy Meatballs.......................................59
Japanese Pork Chops.................................59
Tahini Beef Bites..60
Jamaican Jerk Pork....................................60
Sweet And Sticky Ribs................................60
Cheese & Ham Sliders................................60
Mustard Glazed Pork.................................61
Pork Taquitos..61
Char Siu Buffalo..61
Pork Chilli Cheese Dogs.............................61
Hamburgers With Feta...............................61

Pizza Dogs..62
Chinese Pork With Pineapple......................62
Buttermilk Pork Chops...............................62
Steak Dinner...62
Roast Beef...63
Carne Asada Chips.....................................63
Copycat Burger..63
Pork Schnitzel...63
Beef Kebobs..64
Roast Pork..64
Steak Fajitas...64
Pork Chops With Raspberry And Balsamic....64
Beef Nacho Pinwheels................................65
Homemade Crispy Pepperoni Pizza.............65
Steak Popcorn Bites...................................65

Fish & Seafood Recipes

Chilli Lime Tilapia......................................67
Mushrooms Stuffed With Crab....................67
Thai Fish Cakes...67
Cod Nuggets...68
Lobster Tails..68

Ranch Style Fish Fillets...............................68
Maine Seafood..68
Oat & Parmesan Crusted Fish Fillets............69
Fish Sticks With Tartar Sauce Batter............69
Cajun Shrimp Boil......................................69

Lemon Pepper Shrimp 69
Traditional Fish And Chips 70
Baked Panko Cod..70
Coconut Shrimp 70
Garlic Tilapia 70
Tilapia Fillets 71
Shrimp Wrapped With Bacon 71
Crispy Nacho Prawns.................................71
Crispy Cajun Fish Fingers 71
Beer Battered Fish Tacos 72
Garlic Butter Salmon 72

Thai Salmon Patties 72
Gluten Free Honey And Garlic Shrimp 72
Air Fried Scallops 73
Copycat Fish Fingers 73
Peppery Lemon Shrimp 73
Zesty Fish Fillets 73
Air Fryer Mussels 74
Fish In Foil 74
Store-cupboard Fishcakes 74
Shrimp With Yum Yum Sauce....................74

Desserts Recipes   75

Special Oreos 76
Strawberry Lemonade Pop Tarts................76
Profiteroles 76
Chocolate Mug Cake..................................77
Lemon Tarts 77
Banana Maple Flapjack..............................77
Banana Bread 77
Lava Cakes 78
Fruit Scones 78
Peanut Butter & Chocolate Baked Oats.....78
Oat-covered Banana Fritters 78
Cherry Pies 79
Melting Moments 79
Pecan & Molasses Flapjack 79
Thai Style Bananas 79
Pumpkin Spiced Bread Pudding 80

Cinnamon-maple Pineapple Kebabs..........80
Breakfast Muffins.......................................80
White Chocolate And Raspberry Loaf.......81
Spiced Apples...81
French Toast Sticks 81
Lemon Pies...81
Birthday Cheesecake..................................82
Milk And White Chocolate Chip Air Fryer Donuts
With Frosting 82
Granola...83
Sugar Dough Dippers.................................83
Fruit Crumble...83
Peach Pies 83
Grain-free Millionaire's Shortbread...........84
Apple Chips With Yogurt Dip....................84
Chocolate Eclairs 84

Shopping List   86

APPENDIX A: Measurement Conversions   87

Appendix B : Recipes Index   89

INTRODUCTION

Hello there, I'm Alfie Barrett, and I'm excited to introduce you to my latest culinary creation, the "Instant Vortex Air Fryer Cookbook." As a professional chef with a deep-rooted love for the art of cooking, I've spent years perfecting my skills in kitchens around the world. Throughout my culinary journey, I've come to appreciate the remarkable convenience and versatility of the Instant Vortex Air Fryer. It's a game-changer, and I'm here to guide you on an epic culinary adventure.

The purpose behind this cookbook is straightforward yet profound: to make your cooking experience enjoyable, accessible, and utterly delectable. Whether you're a seasoned chef or just starting your culinary journey, the Instant Vortex Air Fryer has something extraordinary to offer, and this cookbook is your key to unlocking its full potential.

Inside these pages, you'll find a treasure trove of mouthwatering recipes, each carefully crafted for the Instant Vortex Air Fryer. What sets this cookbook apart is the meticulous attention to detail. I've included step-by-step instructions for every dish, complete with cooking times, handy shopping lists, and practical tips that I've honed over my culinary career. It's not just about making cooking easy; it's about elevating your culinary skills.

With the "Instant Vortex Air Fryer Cookbook" by your side, you'll embark on a culinary journey like never before. Whether you're whipping up a quick weekday dinner or impressing guests with gourmet delights, this cookbook is your trusty companion, ensuring that every dish you create is a masterpiece. So, let's dive into the world of air frying together, one delicious recipe at a time. Happy cooking!

Understanding Air Frying

An air fryer operates by using rapid air circulation and intense heat to cook food quickly and create a crispy exterior, mimicking the results of deep frying but with significantly less oil. Inside the air fryer, a heating element heats the air, and a powerful fan circulates this hot air around the food in the cooking basket. As the hot air surrounds the food, it removes moisture

from the surface, which results in the food's outer layer becoming crisp and browned. The heated air also penetrates the food, cooking it thoroughly. The result is a wide range of dishes—from crispy fries to tender chicken—that have a delicious, golden-brown finish and a satisfying crunch, all achieved with minimal oil, making air frying a healthier cooking method compared to traditional deep frying.

Common Cooking Modes for Air Fryers

Air Frying

This is the primary mode of an air fryer. It uses a high-powered fan and a heating element to circulate hot air around the food in the cooking basket. The hot air quickly crisps and browns the food's exterior while cooking it thoroughly. It's perfect for making crispy fries, chicken wings, and other fried favorites with minimal oil.

Roasting

Roasting mode is designed for cooking larger cuts of meat, whole poultry, or vegetables. It uses the same hot air circulation but typically at a slightly lower temperature. This mode helps create a beautifully browned and roasted exterior while keeping the interior moist and flavorful.

Baking

Baking mode in an air fryer is akin to a conventional oven's baking function. It's used for making cakes, muffins, cookies, and other baked goods. The even distribution of heat ensures that your baked items rise and cook uniformly.

Dehydrating

Dehydrating mode uses low temperatures and gentle airflow to remove moisture from foods, effectively preserving them. It's perfect for making dried fruits, beef jerky, or even homemade dried herbs.

Grilling

Some air fryers come equipped with a grill or broil function. In this mode, the heating element is positioned at the top of the appliance, allowing you to grill or broil foods. It's great for achieving grill marks and that delicious charred flavor on items like steaks, burgers, and kebabs.

Reheat

Reheat mode is designed to warm up leftovers or previously cooked dishes quickly. It uses a lower temperature than the original cooking modes to prevent overcooking or further crisping of the food.

Preheat When Necessary: Preheating your air fryer can help improve cooking results, especially for foods that benefit from a crispy exterior. Simply set the air fryer to the desired temperature and let it run for a few minutes before adding your food. This ensures that the hot air is ready to work its magic when you start cooking.

Shake or Flip Food: For even cooking and browning, it's a good practice to shake the basket or flip your food halfway through the cooking time. This ensures that all sides of your food receive the same level of heat and crispiness.

Don't Overcrowd the Basket: To achieve even cooking and optimal crispiness, avoid overcrowding the cooking basket. Give your food some space to allow the hot air to circulate freely. If you're preparing a large batch, cook in multiple batches for the best results.

Check for Doneness: Air fryers cook food quickly, so keep an eye on your dishes to prevent overcooking. Use a meat thermometer to check the internal temperature of meats, ensuring they reach the desired level of doneness. For other items, like vegetables or snacks, check for the desired crispiness and texture.

Use a Light Coating of Oil: While air frying requires less oil than traditional frying, a light coating of oil on your food can enhance its crispiness and flavor. Consider using a cooking spray or a brush to apply a thin layer of oil to items like fries, chicken, or vegetables before air frying.

Experiment and Adapt Recipes: Don't be afraid to experiment with your favorite recipes. Air frying offers a unique cooking method, so feel free to adapt traditional recipes to suit your air fryer. You may need to adjust cooking times and temperatures, but the results can be delicious and healthier.

Bonus Tip: Keep your air fryer clean by regularly removing and washing the cooking basket and accessories, wiping down the interior and exterior, and emptying the crumb tray to prevent smoke and maintain optimal performance.

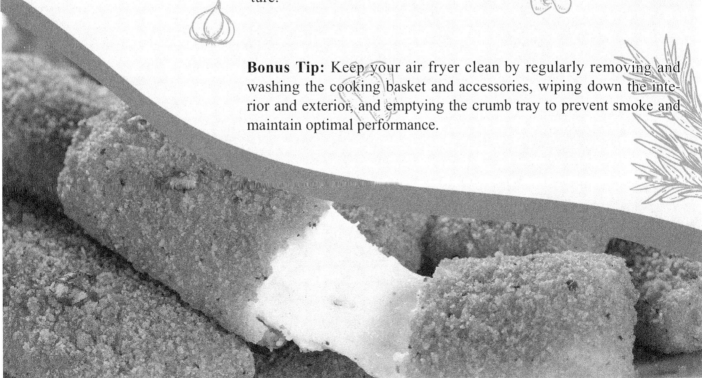

Breakfast & Snacks
And Fries Recipes

Breakfast & Snacks And Fries Recipes

Hard Boiled Eggs Air Fryer Style

Servings: 2
Cooking Time:xx

Ingredients:
- 4 large eggs
- 1 tsp cayenne pepper
- Salt and pepper for seasoning

Directions:
1. Preheat the air fryer to 220°C
2. Take a wire rack and place inside the air fryer
3. Lay the eggs on the rack
4. Cook for between 15-17 minutes, depending upon how you like your eggs
5. Remove from the fryer and place in a bowl of cold water for around 5 minutes
6. Peel and season with the cayenne and the salt and pepper

Easy Air Fryer Sausage

Servings: 5
Cooking Time:xx

Ingredients:
- 5 uncooked sausages
- 1 tbsp mustard
- Salt and pepper for seasoning

Directions:
1. Line the basket of your fryer with parchment paper
2. Arrange the sausages inside the basket
3. Set to 180°C and cook for 15 minutes
4. Turn the sausages over and cook for another 5 minutes
5. Remove and cool
6. Drizzle the mustard over the top and season to your liking

Swede Fries

Servings: 4
Cooking Time:xx

Ingredients:
- 1 medium swede/rutabaga
- ½ teaspoon salt
- ½ teaspoon freshly ground black pepper
- 1½ teaspoons dried thyme
- 1 tablespoon olive oil

Directions:
1. Preheat the air-fryer to 160°C/325°F.
2. Peel the swede/rutabaga and slice into fries about 6 x 1 cm/2½ x ½ in., then toss the fries in the salt, pepper, thyme and oil, making sure every fry is coated.
3. Tip into the preheated air-fryer in a single layer (you may need to cook them in two batches, depending on the size of your air-fryer) and air-fry for 15 minutes, shaking the drawer halfway through. Then increase the temperature to 180°C/350°F and cook for a further 5 minutes. Serve immediately.

Wholegrain Pitta Chips

Servings: 2
Cooking Time:xx

Ingredients:
- 2 round wholegrain pittas, chopped into quarters
- 1 teaspoon olive oil
- ½ teaspoon garlic salt

Directions:
1. Preheat the air-fryer to 180°C/350°F.
2. Spray or brush each pitta quarter with olive oil and sprinkle with garlic salt. Place in the preheated air-fryer and air-fry for 4 minutes, turning halfway through cooking. Serve immediately.

Breakfast Eggs & Spinach

Servings: 4
Cooking Time:xx

Ingredients:
- 500g wilted, fresh spinach
- 200g sliced deli ham
- 1 tbsp olive oil
- 4 eggs
- 4 tsp milk
- Salt and pepper to taste
- 1 tbsp butter for cooking

Directions:
1. Preheat your air fryer to 180ºC
2. You will need 4 small ramekin dishes, coated with a little butter
3. Arrange the wilted spinach, ham, 1 teaspoon of milk and 1 egg into each ramekin and season with a little salt and pepper
4. Place in the fryer 15 to 20 minutes, until the egg is cooked to your liking
5. Allow to cool before serving

Courgette Fries

Servings: 2
Cooking Time:xx

Ingredients:
- 1 courgette/zucchini
- 3 tablespoons plain/all-purpose flour (gluten-free if you wish)
- ¼ teaspoon salt
- ¼ teaspoon freshly ground black pepper
- 60 g/¾ cup dried breadcrumbs (gluten-free if you wish; see page 9)
- 1 teaspoon dried oregano
- 20 g/¼ cup finely grated Parmesan
- 1 egg, beaten

Directions:
1. Preheat the air-fryer to 180ºC/350ºF.
2. Slice the courgette/zucchini into fries about 1.5 x 1.5 x 5 cm/⅝ x ⅝ x 2 in.
3. Season the flour with salt and pepper. Combine the breadcrumbs with the oregano and Parmesan.
4. Dip the courgettes/zucchini in the flour (shaking off any excess flour), then the egg, then the seasoned breadcrumbs.
5. Add the fries to the preheated air-fryer and air-fry for 15 minutes. They should be crispy on the outside but soft on the inside. Serve immediately.

Polenta Fries

Servings: 6
Cooking Time:xx

Ingredients:
- 800 ml/scant 3½ cups water
- 1½ vegetable stock cubes
- ¾ teaspoon dried oregano
- ¾ teaspoon freshly ground black pepper
- 200 g/1⅓ cups quick-cook polenta/cornmeal
- 2 teaspoons olive oil
- 55 g/6 tablespoons plain/all-purpose flour (gluten-free if you wish)
- garlic mayonnaise, to serve

Directions:
1. Bring the water and stock cubes to the boil in a saucepan with the oregano and black pepper. Stir in the polenta/cornmeal and continue to stir until the mixture becomes significantly more solid and is hard to stir – this should take about 5–6 minutes.
2. Grease a 15 x 15-cm/6 x 6-in. baking pan with some of the olive oil. Tip the polenta into the baking pan, smoothing down with the back of a wet spoon. Leave to cool at room temperature for about 30 minutes, then pop into the fridge for at least an hour.
3. Remove the polenta from the fridge and carefully tip out onto a chopping board. Slice the polenta into fingers 7.5 x 1 x 2 cm/3 x ½ x ¾ in. Roll the polenta fingers in the flour, then spray or drizzle the remaining olive oil over the fingers.
4. Preheat the air-fryer to 200ºC/400ºF.
5. Lay the fingers apart from one another in a single layer in the preheated air-fryer (you may need to cook these in batches, depending on the size of your air-fryer). Air-fry for 9 minutes, turning once halfway through cooking. Serve immediately with garlic mayonnaise.

Loaded Hash Browns

Servings: 4
Cooking Time:xx

Ingredients:
- 4 large potatoes
- 2 tbsp bicarbonate of soda
- 1 tbsp salt
- 1 tbsp black pepper
- 1 tsp cayenne pepper
- 2 tbsp olive oil
- 1 large chopped onion
- 1 chopped red pepper
- 1 chopped green pepper

Directions:
1. Grate the potatoes
2. Squeeze out any water contained within the potatoes
3. Take a large bowl of water and add the potatoes
4. Add the bicarbonate of soda, combine everything and leave to soak for 25 minutes
5. Drain the water away and carefully pat the potatoes to dry
6. Transfer your potatoes into another bowl
7. Add the spices and oil
8. Combining everything well, tossing to coat evenly
9. Place your potatoes into your fryer basket
10. Set to 200ºC and cook for 10 minutes
11. Give the potatoes a shake and add the peppers and the onions
12. Cook for another 10 minutes

Potato Fries

Servings: 2
Cooking Time:xx

Ingredients:
- 2 large potatoes (baking potato size)
- 1 teaspoon olive oil
- salt

Directions:
1. Peel the potatoes and slice into fries about 5 x 1.5cm/¾ x ¾ in. by the length of the potato. Submerge the fries in a bowl of cold water and place in the fridge for about 10 minutes.
2. Meanwhile, preheat the air-fryer to 160ºC/325ºF.
3. Drain the fries thoroughly, then toss in the oil and season. Tip into the preheated air-fryer in a single layer (you may need to cook them in two batches, depending on the size of your air-fryer). Air-fry for 15 minutes, tossing once during cooking by shaking the air-fryer drawer, then increase the temperature of the air-fryer to 200ºC/400ºF and cook for a further 3 minutes. Serve immediately.

Oozing Baked Eggs

Servings: 2
Cooking Time:xx

Ingredients:
- 4 eggs
- 140g smoked gouda cheese, cut into small pieces
- Salt and pepper to taste

Directions:
1. You will need two ramekin dishes and spray each one before using
2. Crack two eggs into each ramekin dish
3. Add half of the Gouda cheese to each dish
4. Season and place into the air fryer
5. Cook at 350ºC for 15 minutes, until the eggs are cooked as you like them

Blueberry & Lemon Breakfast Muffins

Servings: 12
Cooking Time:xx

Ingredients:
- 315g self raising flour
- 65g sugar
- 120ml double cream
- 2 tbsp of light cooking oil
- 2 eggs
- 125g blueberries
- The zest and juice of a lemon
- 1 tsp vanilla

Directions:
1. Take a small bowl and mix the self raising flour and sugar together
2. Take another bowl and mix together the oil, juice, eggs, cream, and vanilla
3. Add this mixture to the flour mixture and blend together
4. Add the blueberries and fold
5. You will need individual muffin holders, silicone works best. Spoon the mixture into the holders
6. Cook at 150ºC for 10 minutes
7. Check at the halfway point to check they're not cooking too fast
8. Remove and allow to cool

Morning Sausage Wraps

Servings: 8
Cooking Time:xx

Ingredients:
- 8 sausages, chopped into pieces
- 2 slices of cheddar cheese, cut into quarters
- 1 can of regular crescent roll dough
- 8 wooden skewers

Directions:
1. Take the dough and separate each one
2. Cut open the sausages evenly
3. The one of your crescent rolls and on the widest part, add a little sausage and then a little cheese
4. Roll the dough and tuck it until you form a triangle
5. Repeat this for four times and add into your air fryer
6. Cook at 190ºC for 3 minutes
7. Remove your dough and add a skewer for serving
8. Repeat with the other four pieces of dough

Cumin Shoestring Carrots

Servings: 2
Cooking Time:xx

Ingredients:
- 300 g/10½ oz. carrots
- 1 teaspoon cornflour/cornstarch
- 1 teaspoon ground cumin
- ¼ teaspoon salt
- 1 tablespoon olive oil
- garlic mayonnaise, to serve

Directions:
1. Preheat the air-fryer to 200ºC/400ºF.
2. Peel the carrots and cut into thin fries, roughly 10 cm x 1 cm x 5 mm/4 x ½ x ¼ in. Toss the carrots in a bowl with all the other ingredients.
3. Add the carrots to the preheated air-fryer and air-fry for 9 minutes, shaking the drawer of the air-fryer a couple of times during cooking. Serve with garlic mayo on the side.

Easy Cheese & Bacon Toasties

Servings: 2
Cooking Time:xx

Ingredients:
- 4 slices of sandwich bread
- 2 slices of cheddar cheese
- 5 slices of pre-cooked bacon
- 1 tbsp melted butter
- 2 slices of mozzarella cheese

Directions:
1. Take the bread and spread the butter onto one side of each slice
2. Place one slice of bread into the fryer basket, buttered side facing downwards
3. Place the cheddar on top, followed by the bacon, mozzarella and the other slice of bread on top, buttered side upwards
4. Set your fryer to 170ºC
5. Cook for 4 minutes and then turn over and cook for another 3 minutes
6. Serve whilst still hot

Your Favourite Breakfast Bacon

Servings: 2
Cooking Time:xx

Ingredients:
- 4-5 rashers of lean bacon, fat cut off
- Salt and pepper for seasoning

Directions:
1. Line your air fryer basket with parchment paper
2. Place the bacon in the basket
3. Set the fryer to 200ºC
4. Cook for 10 minutes for crispy. If you want it very crispy, cook for another 2 minutes

Delicious Breakfast Casserole

Servings: 4
Cooking Time:xx

Ingredients:
- 4 frozen hash browns
- 8 sausages, cut into pieces
- 4 eggs
- 1 diced yellow pepper
- 1 diced green pepper
- 1 diced red pepper
- Half a diced onion

Directions:
1. Line the bottom of your fryer with aluminium foil and arrange the hash browns inside
2. Add the sausage on top (uncooked)
3. Now add the onions and the peppers, sprinkling evenly
4. Cook the casserole on 170ºC for around 10 minutes
5. Open your fryer and give the mixture a good stir

6. Combine the eggs in a small bowl and pour over the casserole, closing the lid

7. Cook for another 10 minutes on the same temperature

8. Serve with a little seasoning to taste

French Toast

Servings: 2
Cooking Time:xx

Ingredients:
- 2 beaten eggs
- 2 tbsp softened butter
- 4 slices of sandwich bread
- 1 tsp cinnamon
- 1 tsp nutmeg
- 1 tsp ground cloves
- 1 tsp maple syrup

Directions:

1. Preheat your fryer to 180ºC

2. Take a bowl and add the eggs, salt, cinnamon, nutmeg, and cloves, combining well

3. Take your bread and butter each side, cutting into strips

4. Dip the bread slices into the egg mixture

5. Arrange each slice into the basket of your fryer

6. Cook for 2 minutes

7. Take the basket out and spray with a little cooking spray

8. Turn over the slices and place back into the fryer

9. Cook for 4 minutes

10. Remove and serve with maple syrup

Monte Cristo Breakfast Sandwich

Servings: 4
Cooking Time:xx

Ingredients:
- 1 egg
- 2 slices of sandwich bread
- 1/4 tsp vanilla extract
- 4 slices of sliced Swiss cheese
- 4 slices of sliced deli ham
- 4 slices of sliced turkey
- 1 tsp melted butter
- Powdered sugar for serving

Directions:

1. In a small bowl, mix together the egg and vanilla extract, combining well

2. Take your bread and assemble your sandwich, starting with a slice of cheese, then the ham, turkey, and then another slice of the cheese, with the other slice of bread on the top

3. Compress the sandwich a little, so it cooks better

4. Take a piece of cooking foil and brush over it with the butter

5. Take your sandwich and dip each side into the egg mixture, leaving it to one side for around half a minute

6. Place the sandwich on the foil and place it inside your fryer

7. Cook at 200ºC for around 10 minutes, before turning the sandwich over and cooking for another 8 minutes

8. Transfer your sandwich onto a plate and sprinkle with a little powdered sugar

Crunchy Mexican Breakfast Wrap

Servings: 2
Cooking Time:xx

Ingredients:
- 2 large tortillas
- 2 corn tortillas
- 1 sliced jalapeño pepper
- 4 tbsp ranchero sauce
- 1 sliced avocado
- 25g cooked pinto beans

Directions:

1. Take each of your large tortillas and add the egg, jalapeño, sauce, the corn tortillas, the avocado and the pinto beans, in that order. If you want to add more sauce at this point, you can

2. Fold over your wrap to make sure that nothing escapes

3. Place each wrap into your fryer and cook at 190ºC for 6 minutes

4. Remove your wraps and place in the oven, cooking for a further 5 minutes at 180ºC, until crispy

5. Place each wrap into a frying pan and crisp a little more on a low heat, for a couple of minutes on each side

Healthy Stuffed Peppers

Servings: 2
Cooking Time:xx

Ingredients:
- 1 large bell pepper, deseeded and cut into halves
- 1 tsp olive oil
- 4 large eggs
- Salt and pepper to taste

Directions:
1. Take your peppers and rub a little olive oil on the edges
2. Into each pepper, crack one egg and season with salt and pepper
3. You will need to insert a trivet into your air fryer to hold the peppers, and then arrange the peppers evenly
4. Set your fryer to 200ºC and cook for 13 minutes
5. Once cooked, remove and serve with a little more seasoning, if required

Mexican Breakfast Burritos

Servings: 6
Cooking Time:xx

Ingredients:
- 6 scrambled eggs
- 6 medium tortillas
- Half a minced red pepper
- 8 sausages, cut into cubes and browned
- 4 pieces of bacon, pre-cooked and cut into pieces
- 65g grated cheese of your choice
- A small amount of olive oil for cooking

Directions:
1. Into a regular mixing bowl, combine the eggs, bell pepper, bacon pieces, the cheese, and the browned sausage, giving everything a good stir
2. Take your first tortilla and place half a cup of the mixture into the middle, folding up the top and bottom and rolling closed
3. Repeat until all your tortillas have been used
4. Arrange the burritos into the bottom of your fryer and spray with a little oil
5. Cook the burritos at 170ºC for 5 minutes

Easy Cheesy Scrambled Eggs

Servings: 1
Cooking Time:xx

Ingredients:
- 1 tbsp butter
- 2 eggs
- 100g grated cheese
- 2 tbsp milk
- Salt and pepper for seasoning

Directions:
1. Add the butter inside the air fryer pan and cook at 220ºC until the butter has melted
2. Add the eggs and milk to a bowl and combine, seasoning to your liking
3. Pour the eggs into the butter panned cook for 3 minutes, stirring around lightly to scramble
4. Add the cheese and cook for another 2 more minutes

Avocado Fries

Servings: 2
Cooking Time:xx

Ingredients:
- 35 g/¼ cup plain/all-purpose flour (gluten free if you wish)
- ½ teaspoon chilli/chili powder
- 1 egg, beaten
- 50 g/heaped ½ cup dried breadcrumbs (gluten-free if you wish; see page 9)
- 1 avocado, skin and stone removed, and each half sliced lengthways
- salt and freshly ground black pepper

Directions:
1. Preheat the air-fryer to 200ºC/400ºF.
2. In a bowl combine the flour and chilli/chili powder, then season with salt and pepper. Place the beaten egg in a second bowl and the breadcrumbs in a third bowl.
3. Dip each avocado slice in the seasoned flour (shaking off any excess), then the egg and finally the breadcrumbs.
4. Add the breaded avocado slices to the preheated air-fryer and air-fry for 6 minutes, turning after 4 minutes. Serve immediately.

Egg & Bacon Breakfast Cups

Servings: 8
Cooking Time:xx

Ingredients:
- 6 eggs
- 1 chopped red pepper
- 1 chopped green pepper
- 1 chopped yellow pepper
- 2 tbsp double cream
- 50g chopped spinach
- 50g grated cheddar cheese
- 50g grated mozzarella cheese
- 3 slices of cooked bacon, crumbled into pieces

Directions:
1. Take a large mixing bowl and crack the eggs
2. Add the cream and season with a little salt and pepper, combining everything well
3. Add the peppers, spinach, onions, both cheeses, and the crumbled bacon, combining everything once more
4. You will need silicone moulds or cups for this part, and you should pour equal amounts of the mixture into 8 cups
5. Cook at 150ºC for around 12 or 15 minutes, until the eggs are cooked properly

Cheesy Sausage Breakfast Pockets

Servings: 2
Cooking Time:xx

Ingredients:
- 1 packet of regular puff pastry
- 4 sausages, cooked and crumbled into pieces
- 5 eggs
- 50g cooked bacon
- 50g grated cheddar cheese

Directions:
1. Scramble your eggs in your usual way
2. Add the sausage and the bacon as you are cooking the eggs and combine well
3. Take your pastry sheets and cut rectangular shapes
4. Add a little of the egg and meat mixture to one half of each pastry piece
5. Fold the rectangles over and use a fork to seal down the edges
6. Place your pockets into your air fryer and cook at 190ºC for 10 minutes
7. Allow to cool before serving

Bocconcini Balls

Servings: 2
Cooking Time:xx

Ingredients:
- 70 g/½ cup plus ½ tablespoon plain/all-purpose flour (gluten-free if you wish)
- 1 egg, beaten
- 70 g/1 cup dried breadcrumbs (gluten-free if you wish; see page 9)
- 10 bocconcini

Directions:
1. Preheat the air-fryer to 200ºC/400ºF.
2. Place the flour, egg and breadcrumbs on 3 separate plates. Dip each bocconcini ball first in the flour to coat, then the egg, shaking off any excess before rolling in the breadcrumbs.
3. Add the breaded bocconcini to the preheated air-fryer and air-fry for 5 minutes (no need to turn them during cooking). Serve immediately.

Pitta Pizza

Servings: 2
Cooking Time:xx

Ingredients:
- 2 round wholemeal pitta breads
- 3 tablespoons passata/strained tomatoes
- 4 tablespoons grated mozzarella
- 1 teaspoon dried oregano
- 1 teaspoon olive oil
- basil leaves, to serve

Directions:
1. Preheat the air-fryer to 200ºC/400ºF.
2. Pop the pittas into the preheated air-fryer and air-fry for 1 minute.
3. Remove the pittas from the air-fryer and spread a layer of the passata/strained tomatoes on the pittas, then scatter over the mozzarella, oregano and oil. Return to the air-fryer and air-fry for a further 4 minutes. Scatter over the basil leaves and serve immediately.

Blanket Breakfast Eggs

Servings: 2
Cooking Time:xx

Ingredients:

- 2 eggs
- 2 slices of sandwich bread
- Olive oil spray
- Salt and pepper to taste

Directions:

1. Preheat your air fryer to 190ºC and spray with a little oil
2. Meanwhile, take your bread and cut a hole into the middle of each piece
3. Place one slice inside your fryer and crack one egg into the middle
4. Season with a little salt and pepper
5. Cook for 5 minutes, before turning over and cooking for a further 2 minutes
6. Remove the first slice and repeat the process with the remaining slice of bread and egg

Blueberry Bread

Servings: 8
Cooking Time:xx

Ingredients:

- 260ml milk
- 3 eggs
- 25g protein powder
- 400g frozen blueberries
- 600g bisquick or pancake mixture

Directions:

1. Take a large mixing bowl and combine all ingredients until smooth
2. Preheat the air fryer to 250ºC
3. Place the mixture into a loaf tin
4. Place the tin into the air fryer and cook for 30 minutes
5. A toothpick should come out clean if the bread is cooked

Easy Omelette

Servings: 1
Cooking Time:xx

Ingredients:

- 50ml milk
- 2 eggs
- 60g grated cheese, any you like
- Any garnishes you like, such as mushrooms, peppers, etc.

Directions:

1. Take a small mixing bowl and crack the eggs inside, whisking with the milk
2. Add the salt and garnishes and combine again
3. Grease a 6x3" pan and pour the mixture inside
4. Arrange the pan inside the air fryer basket
5. Cook at 170ºC for 10 minutes
6. At the halfway point, sprinkle the cheese on top
7. Loosen the edges with a spatula before serving

Breakfast Sausage Burgers

Servings: 2
Cooking Time:xx

Ingredients:

- 8 links of your favourite sausage
- Salt and pepper to taste

Directions:

1. Remove the sausage from the skins and use a fork to create a smooth mixture
2. Season to your liking
3. Shape the sausage mixture into burgers or patties
4. Preheat your air fryer to 260ºC
5. Arrange the burgers in the fryer, so they are not touching each other
6. Cook for 8 minutes
7. Serve still warm

Sauces & Snack And Appetiser Recipes

Sauces & Snack And Appetiser Recipes

Spring Rolls

Servings: 20
Cooking Time:xx

Ingredients:
- 160g dried rice noodles
- 1 tsp sesame oil
- 300g minced beef
- 200g frozen vegetables
- 1 onion, diced
- 3 cloves garlic, crushed
- 1 tsp soy sauce
- 1 tbsp vegetable oil
- 1 pack egg roll wrappers

Directions:
1. Soak the noodles in a bowl of water until soft
2. Add the minced beef, onion, garlic and vegetables to a pan and cook for 6 minutes
3. Remove from the heat, stir in the noodles and add the soy
4. Heat the air fryer to 175°C
5. Add a diagonal strip of filling in each egg roll wrapper
6. Fold the top corner over the filling, fold in the two side corners
7. Brush the centre with water and roll to seal
8. Brush with vegetable oil, place in the air fryer and cook for about 8 minutes until browned

Beetroot Crisps

Servings: 2
Cooking Time:xx

Ingredients:
- 3 medium beetroots
- 2 tbsp oil
- Salt to taste

Directions:
1. Peel and thinly slice the beetroot
2. Coat with the oil and season with salt
3. Preheat the air fryer to 200°C
4. Place in the air fryer and cook for 12-18 minutes until crispy

Sweet Potato Crisps

Servings: 4
Cooking Time:xx

Ingredients:
- 1 sweet potato, peeled and thinly sliced
- 2 tbsp oil
- ¼ tsp salt
- ¼ tsp pepper
- 1 tsp chopped rosemary
- Cooking spray

Directions:
1. Place all ingredients in a bowl and mix well
2. Place in the air fryer and cook at 175°C for about 15 minutes until crispy

Snack Style Falafel

Servings: 15
Cooking Time:xx

Ingredients:
- 150g dry garbanzo beans
- 300g coriander
- 75g flat leaf parsley
- 1 red onion, quartered
- 1 clove garlic
- 2 tbsp chickpea flour
- Cooking spray
- 1 tbsp cumin
- 1 tbsp coriander
- 1 tbsp sriracha
- ½ tsp baking powder
- Salt and pepper to taste
- ¼ tsp baking soda

Directions:
1. Add all ingredients apart from the baking soda and baking powder to a food processor and blend well
2. Cover and rest for 1 hour
3. Heat air fryer to 190°C
4. Add baking powder and baking soda to mix and combine
5. Form mix into 15 equal balls
6. Spray air fryer with cooking spray
7. Add to air fryer and cook for 8-10 minutes

Garlic Cheese Bread

Servings: 2
Cooking Time:xx

Ingredients:
- 250g grated mozzarella
- 50g grated parmesan
- 1 egg
- ½ tsp garlic powder

Directions:
1. Line air fryer with parchment paper
2. Mix ingredients in a bowl
3. Press into a circle onto the parchment paper in the air fryer
4. Heat the air fryer to 175°C
5. Cook for 10 minutes

Pao De Queijo

Servings: 20
Cooking Time:xx

Ingredients:
- 150g sweet starch
- 150g sour starch
- 50ml milk
- 25ml water
- 25ml olive oil
- 1 tsp salt
- 2 eggs
- 100g grated cheese
- 50g grated parmesan

Directions:
1. Preheat the air fryer to 170°C
2. Mix the starch together in a bowl until well mixed
3. Add olive oil, milk and water to a pan, bring to the boil and reduce the heat
4. Add the starch and mix until all the liquid is absorbed
5. Add the eggs and mix to a dough
6. Add the cheeses and mix well
7. Form the dough into balls
8. Line the air fryer with parchment paper
9. Bake in the air fryer for 8-10 minutes

Lumpia

Servings: 16
Cooking Time:xx

Ingredients:
- 400g Italian sausage
- 1 sliced onion
- 1 chopped carrot
- 50g chopped water chestnuts
- Cooking spray
- 2 cloves minced, garlic
- 2 tbsp soy sauce
- ½ tsp salt
- ¼ tsp ground ginger
- 16 spring roll wrappers

Directions:
1. Cook sausage in a pan for about 5 minutes. Add green onions, onions, water chestnuts and carrot cook for 7 minutes
2. Add garlic and cook for a further 2 minutes
3. Add the soy sauce, salt and ginger, stir to mix well
4. Add filling to each spring roll wrapper.
5. Roll over the bottom and tuck in the sides, continue to roll up the spring roll
6. Spray with cooking spray and place in the air fryer
7. Cook at 200°C for 4 minutes turn and cook for a further 4 minutes

Jalapeño Poppers

Servings: 2
Cooking Time:xx

Ingredients:
- 10 jalapeños, halved and deseeded
- 100g cream cheese
- 50g parsley
- 150g breadcrumbs

Directions:
1. Mix 1/2 the breadcrumbs with the cream cheese
2. Add the parsley
3. Stuff the peppers with the cream cheese mix
4. Top the peppers with the remaining breadcrumbs
5. Heat the air fryer to 185°C
6. Place in the air fryer and cook for 6-8 minutes

Tortellini Bites

Servings: 6
Cooking Time:xx

Ingredients:

- 200g cheese tortellini
- 150g flour
- 100g panko bread crumbs
- 50g grated parmesan
- 1 tsp dried oregano
- 2 eggs
- ½ tsp garlic powder
- ½ tsp chilli flakes
- Salt
- Pepper

Directions:

1. Cook the tortellini according to the packet instructions
2. Mix the panko, parmesan, oregano, garlic powder, chilli flakes salt and pepper in a bowl
3. Beat the eggs in another bowl and place the flour in a third bowl
4. Coat the tortellini in flour, then egg and then in the panko mix
5. Place in the air fryer and cook at 185ºC for 10 minutes until crispy
6. Serve with marinara sauce for dipping

Popcorn Tofu

Servings: 4
Cooking Time:xx

Ingredients:

- 400g firm tofu
- 100g chickpea flour
- 100g oatmeal
- 2 tbsp yeast
- 150ml milk
- 400g breadcrumbs
- 1 tsp garlic powder
- 1 tsp onion powder
- 1 tbsp dijon mustard
- ½ tsp salt
- ½ tsp pepper
- 2 tbsp vegetable bouillon

Directions:

1. Rip the tofu into pieces. Place the breadcrumbs into a bowl, in another bowl mix the remaining ingredients
2. Dip the tofu into the batter mix and then dip into the breadcrumbs
3. Heat the air fryer to 175ºC
4. Place the tofu in the air fryer and cook for 12 minutes shaking halfway through

Mac & Cheese Bites

Servings: 14
Cooking Time:xx

Ingredients:

- 200g mac and cheese
- 2 eggs
- 200g panko breadcrumbs
- Cooking spray

Directions:

1. Place drops of mac and cheese on parchment paper and freeze for 1 hour
2. Beat the eggs in a bowl, add the breadcrumbs to another bowl
3. Dip the mac and cheese balls in the egg then into the breadcrumbs
4. Heat the air fryer to 190ºC
5. Place in the air fryer, spray with cooking spray and cook for 15 minutes

Korean Chicken Wings

Servings: 2
Cooking Time:xx

Ingredients:

- 25ml soy sauce
- 40g brown sugar
- 2 tbsp hot pepper paste
- 1 tsp sesame oil
- ½ tsp ginger paste
- ½ tsp garlic paste
- 2 green onions, chopped
- 400g chicken wings
- 1 tbsp vegetable oil

Directions:

1. Preheat air fryer to 200ºC
2. Place all ingredients apart from chicken wings and vegetable oil in a pan and simmer for about 4 minutes set aside
3. Massage the vegetable oil into the chicken wings
4. Place in the air fryer and cook for about 10 minutes
5. Turn and cook for a further 10 minutes
6. Coat the wings in the sauce and return to the air fryer
7. Cook for about 2 minutes

Air-fried Pickles

Servings: 4
Cooking Time:xx

Ingredients:
- 1/2 cup mayonnaise
- 2 tsp sriracha sauce
- 1 jar dill pickle slices
- 1 egg
- 2 tbsp milk
- 50g flour
- 50g cornmeal
- ½ tsp seasoned salt
- ¼ tsp paprika
- ¼ tsp garlic powder
- ⅛ tsp pepper
- Cooking spray

Directions:
1. Mix the mayo and sriracha together in a bowl and set aside
2. Heat the air fryer to 200ºC
3. Drain the pickles and pat dry
4. Mix egg and milk together, in another bowl mix all the remaining ingredients
5. Dip the pickles in the egg mix then in the flour mix
6. Spray the air fryer with cooking spray
7. Cook for about 4 minutes until crispy

Onion Bahji

Servings: 8
Cooking Time:xx

Ingredients:
- 1 sliced red onion
- 1 sliced onion
- 1 tsp salt
- 1 minced jalapeño pepper
- 150g chickpea flour
- 4 tbsp water
- 1 clove garlic, minced
- 1 tsp coriander
- 1 tsp chilli powder
- 1 tsp turmeric
- ½ tsp cumin

Directions:
1. Place all ingredients in a bowl and mix well, leave to rest for 10 minutes
2. Preheat air fryer to 175ºC
3. Spray air fryer with cooking spray.
4. Form mix into bahji shapes and add to air fryer
5. Cook for 6 minutes turn and cook for a further 6 minutes

Bacon Smokies

Servings: 8
Cooking Time:xx

Ingredients:
- 150g little smokies (pieces)
- 150g bacon
- 50g brown sugar
- Toothpicks

Directions:
1. Cut the bacon strips into thirds
2. Put the brown sugar into a bowl
3. Coat the bacon with the sugar
4. Wrap the bacon around the little smokies and secure with a toothpick
5. Heat the air fryer to 170ºC
6. Place in the air fryer and cook for 10 minutes until crispy

Salt And Vinegar Chickpeas

Servings: 5
Cooking Time:xx

Ingredients:
- 1 can chickpeas
- 100ml white vinegar
- 1 tbsp olive oil
- Salt to taste

Directions:
1. Combine chickpeas and vinegar in a pan, simmer remove from heat and stand for 30 minutes
2. Preheat the air fryer to 190ºC
3. Drain chickpeas
4. Place chickpeas in the air fryer and cook for about 4 minutes
5. Pour chickpeas into an ovenproof bowl drizzle with oil, sprinkle with salt
6. Place bowl in the air fryer and cook for another 4 minutes

Mozzarella Sticks

Servings: 4
Cooking Time:xx

Ingredients:
- 60ml water
- 50g flour
- 5 tbsp cornstarch
- 1 tbsp cornmeal
- 1 tsp garlic powder
- ½ tsp salt
- 100g breadcrumbs
- ½ tsp pepper
- ½ tsp parsley
- ½ tsp onion powder
- ¼ tsp oregano
- ½ tsp basil
- 200g mozzarella cut into ½ inch strips

Directions:
1. Mix water, flour, cornstarch, cornmeal, garlic powder and salt in a bowl
2. Stir breadcrumbs, pepper, parsley, onion powder, oregano and basil together in another bowl
3. Dip the mozzarella sticks in the batter then coat in the breadcrumbs
4. Heat the air fryer to 200ºC
5. Cook for 6 minutes turn and cook for another 6 minutes

Peppers With Aioli Dip

Servings: 4
Cooking Time:xx

Ingredients:
- 250g shishito peppers
- 2 tsp avocado oil
- 5 tbsp mayonnaise
- 2 tbsp lemon juice
- 1 minced clove of garlic
- 1 tbsp chopped parsley
- Salt and pepper for seasoning

Directions:
1. Take a medium bowl and combine the mayonnaise with the lemon juice, garlic, parsley and seasoning and create a smooth dip
2. Preheat the air fryer to 220ºC
3. Toss the peppers in the oil and add to the air fryer
4. Cook for 4 minutes, until the peppers are soft and blistered on the outside

5. Remove and serve with the dip

Pork Jerky

Servings: 35
Cooking Time:xx

Ingredients:
- 300g mince pork
- 1 tbsp oil
- 1 tbsp sriracha
- 1 tbsp soy
- ½ tsp pink curing salt
- 1 tbsp rice vinegar
- ½ tsp salt
- ½ tsp pepper
- ½ tsp onion powder

Directions:
1. Mix all ingredients in a bowl until combined
2. Refrigerate for about 8 hours
3. Shape into sticks and place in the air fryer
4. Heat the air fryer to 160ºC
5. Cook for 1 hour turn then cook for another hour
6. Turn again and cook for another hour
7. Cover with paper and sit for 8 hours

Spicy Peanuts

Servings: 8
Cooking Time:xx

Ingredients:
- 2 tbsp olive oil
- 3 tbsp seafood seasoning
- ½ tsp cayenne
- 300g raw peanuts
- Salt to taste

Directions:
1. Preheat the air fryer to 160ºC
2. Whisk together ingredients in a bowl and stir in the peanuts
3. Add to air fryer and cook for 10 minutes, shake then cook for a further 10 minutes
4. Sprinkle with salt and cook for another 5 minutes

Onion Pakoda

Servings: 2
Cooking Time:xx

Ingredients:
- 200g gram flour
- 2 onions, thinly sliced
- 1 tbsp crushed coriander seeds
- 1 tsp chilli powder
- ¾ tsp salt
- ¼ tsp turmeric
- ¼ tsp baking soda

Directions:
1. Mix all the ingredients together in a large bowl
2. Make bite sized pakodas
3. Heat the air fryer to 200ºC
4. Line the air fryer with foil
5. Place the pakoda in the air fryer and cook for 5 minutes
6. Turn over and cook for a further 5 minutes

Tostones

Servings: 4
Cooking Time:xx

Ingredients:
- 2 unripe plantains
- Olive oil cooking spray
- 300ml of water
- Salt to taste

Directions:
1. Preheat the air fryer to 200ºC
2. Slice the tips off the plantain
3. Cut the plantain into 1 inch chunks
4. Place in the air fryer spray with oil and cook for 5 minutes
5. Remove the plantain from the air fryer and smash to ½ inch pieces
6. Soak in a bowl of salted water
7. Remove from the water and return to the air fryer season with salt cook for 5 minutes
8. Turn and cook for another 5 minutes

Cheese Wontons

Servings: 8
Cooking Time:xx

Ingredients:
- 8 wonton wrappers
- 1 carton pimento cheese
- Small dish of water
- Cooking spray

Directions:
1. Place one tsp of cheese in the middle of each wonton wrapper
2. Brush the edges of each wonton wrapper with water
3. Fold over to create a triangle and seal
4. Heat the air fryer to 190ºC
5. Spray the wontons with cooking spray
6. Place in the air fryer and cook for 3 minutes
7. Turnover and cook for a further 3 minutes

Pepperoni Bread

Servings: 4
Cooking Time:xx

Ingredients:
- Cooking spray
- 400g pizza dough
- 200g pepperoni
- 1 tbsp dried oregano
- Ground pepper to taste
- Garlic salt to taste
- 1 tsp melted butter
- 1 tsp grated parmesan
- 50g grated mozzarella

Directions:
1. Line a baking tin with 2 inch sides with foil to fit in the air fryer
2. Spray with cooking spray
3. Preheat the air fryer to 200ºC
4. Roll the pizza dough into 1 inch balls and line the baking tin
5. Sprinkle with pepperoni, oregano, pepper and garlic salt
6. Brush with melted butter and sprinkle with parmesan
7. Place in the air fryer and cook for 15 minutes
8. Sprinkle with mozzarella and cook for another 2 minutes

Salt And Vinegar Chips

Servings: 4
Cooking Time:xx

Ingredients:
- 6-10 Jerusalem artichokes, thinly sliced
- 150ml apple cider vinegar
- 2 tbsp olive oil
- Sea salt

Directions:
1. Soak the artichoke in apple cider vinegar for 20-30 minutes
2. Preheat the air fryer to 200ºC
3. Coat the artichoke in olive oil
4. Place in the air fryer and cook for 15 Minutes
5. Sprinkle with salt

Jalapeño Pockets

Servings: 4
Cooking Time:xx

Ingredients:
- 1 chopped onion
- 60g cream cheese
- 1 jalapeño, chopped
- 8 wonton wrappers
- ¼ tsp garlic powder
- ⅛ tsp onion powder

Directions:
1. Cook the onion in a pan for 5 minutes until softened
2. Add to a bowl and mix with the remaining ingredients
3. Lay the wonton wrappers out and add filling to each one
4. Fold over to create a triangle and seal with water around the edges
5. Heat the air fryer to 200ºC
6. Place in the air fryer and cook for about 4 minutes

Asian Devilled Eggs

Servings: 12
Cooking Time:xx

Ingredients:
- 6 large eggs
- 2 tbsp mayo
- 1 ½ tsp sriracha
- 1 ½ tsp sesame oil
- 1 tsp soy sauce
- 1 tsp dijon mustard
- 1 tsp finely grated ginger
- 1 tsp rice vinegar
- 1 chopped green onion
- Toasted sesame seeds

Directions:
1. Set air fryer to 125ºC
2. Place eggs in the air fryer and cook for 15 minutes
3. Remove from the air fryer and place in a bowl of iced water for 10 minutes
4. Peel and cut in half
5. Scoop out the yolks and place in a food processor
6. Add the ingredients apart from the sesame seeds and green onion and combine until smooth
7. Place in a piping bag and pipe back into the egg whites
8. Garnish with seeds and green onion

Stuffed Mushrooms

Servings: 24
Cooking Time:xx

Ingredients:
- 24 mushrooms
- ½ pepper, sliced
- ½ diced onion
- 1 small carrot, diced
- 200g grated cheese
- 2 slices bacon, diced
- 100g sour cream

Directions:
1. Place the mushroom stems, pepper, onion, carrot and bacon in a pan and cook for about 5 minutes
2. Stir in cheese and sour cream, cook until well combined
3. Heat the air fryer to 175ºC
4. Add stuffing to each of the mushrooms
5. Place in the air fryer and cook for 8 minutes

Pretzel Bites

Servings: 2
Cooking Time:xx

Ingredients:
- 650g flour
- 2.5 tsp active dry yeast
- 260ml hot water
- 1 tsp salt
- 4 tbsp melted butter
- 2 tbsp sugar

Directions:
1. Take a large bowl and add the flour, sugar and salt
2. Take another bowl and combine the hot water and yeast, stirring until the yeast has dissolved
3. Then, add the yeast mixture to the flour mixture and use your hands to combine
4. Knead for 2 minutes
5. Cover the bowl with a kitchen towel for around half an hour
6. Divide the dough into 6 pieces
7. Preheat the air fryer to 260ºC
8. Take each section of dough and tear off a piece, rolling it in your hands to create a rope shape, that is around 1" in thickness
9. Cut into 2" strips
10. Place the small dough balls into the air fryer and leave a little space in-between
11. Cook for 6 minutes
12. Once cooked, remove and brush with melted butter and sprinkle salt on top

Pasta Chips

Servings: 2
Cooking Time:xx

Ingredients:
- 300g dry pasta bows
- 1 tbsp olive oil
- 1 tbsp nutritional yeast
- 1½ tsp Italian seasoning
- ½ tsp salt

Directions:
1. Cook the pasta for half the time stated on the packet
2. Drain and mix with the oil, yeast, seasoning and salt
3. Place in the air fryer and cook at 200ºC for 5 minutes shake and cook for a further 3 minutes until crunchy

Thai Bites

Servings: 4
Cooking Time:xx

Ingredients:
- 400g pork mince
- 1 onion
- 1 tsp garlic paste
- 1 tbsp soy
- 1 tbsp Worcester sauce
- Salt and pepper
- 2 tsp Thai curry paste
- ½ lime juice and zest
- 1 tsp mixed spice
- 1 tsp Chinese spice
- 1 tsp coriander

Directions:
1. Place all ingredients in a bowl and mix well
2. Shape into balls
3. Place in the air fryer and cook at 180ºC for 15 minutes

Vegetarian & Vegan Recipes

Vegetarian & Vegan Recipes

Roasted Vegetable Pasta

Servings:4
Cooking Time:15 Minutes

Ingredients:
- 400 g / 14 oz penne pasta
- 1 courgette, sliced
- 1 red pepper, deseeded and sliced
- 100 g / 3.5 oz mushroom, sliced
- 2 tbsp olive oil
- 1 tsp Italian seasoning
- 200 g cherry tomatoes, halved
- 2 tbsp fresh basil, chopped
- ½ tsp black pepper

Directions:
1. Cook the pasta according to the packet instructions.
2. Preheat the air fryer to 190 °C / 370 °F and line the air fryer with parchment paper or grease it with olive oil.
3. In a bowl, place the courgette, pepper, and mushroom, and toss in 2 tbsp olive oil
4. Place the vegetables in the air fryer and cook for 15 minutes.
5. Once the vegetables have softened, mix with the penne pasta, chopped cherry tomatoes, and fresh basil.
6. Serve while hot with a sprinkle of black pepper in each dish.

Potato Gratin

Servings: 4
Cooking Time:xx

Ingredients:
- 2 large potatoes
- 2 beaten eggs
- 100ml coconut cream
- 1 tbsp plain flour
- 50g grated cheddar

Directions:
1. Slice the potatoes into thin slices, place in the air fryer and cook for 10 minutes at 180ºC
2. Mix eggs, coconut cream and flour together
3. Line four ramekins with the potato slices
4. Cover with the cream mixture, sprinkle with cheese and cook for 10 minutes at 200ºC

Pakoras

Servings: 8
Cooking Time:xx

Ingredients:
- 200g chopped cauliflower
- 100g diced pepper
- 250g chickpea flour
- 30ml water
- ½ tsp cumin
- Cooking spray
- 1 onion, diced
- 1 tsp salt
- 1 garlic clove, minced
- 1 tsp curry powder
- 1 tsp coriander
- ½ tsp cayenne

Directions:
1. Preheat air fryer to 175ºC
2. Place all ingredients in a bowl and mix well
3. Spray cooking basket with oil
4. Spoon 2 tbsp of mix into the basket and flatten, continue until the basket is full
5. Cook for 8 minutes, turn then cook for a further 8 minutes

Courgette Burgers

Servings: 4
Cooking Time:xx

Ingredients:
- 1 courgette
- 1 small can of chickpeas, drained
- 3 spring onions
- Pinch of dried garlic
- Salt and pepper
- 3 tbsp coriander
- 1 tsp chilli powder
- 1 tsp mixed spice
- 1 tsp cumin

Directions:
1. Grate the courgette and drain the excess water
2. Thinly slice the spring onions and add to the bowl with the chickpeas, courgette and seasoning
3. Bind the ingredients and form into patties
4. Place in the air fryer and cook for 12 minutes at 200ºC

Spring Ratatouille

Servings:2
Cooking Time:15 Minutes

Ingredients:
- 1 tbsp olive oil
- 4 Roma tomatoes, sliced
- 2 cloves garlic, minced
- 1 courgette, cut into chunks
- 1 red pepper and 1 yellow pepper, cut into chunks
- 2 tbsp mixed herbs
- 1 tbsp vinegar

Directions:
1. Preheat the air fryer to 190 °C / 370 °F and line the air fryer with parchment paper or grease it with olive oil.
2. Place all of the ingredients into a large mixing bowl and mix until fully combined.
3. Transfer the vegetables into the lined air fryer basket, close the lid, and cook for 15 minutes until the vegetables have softened.

Onion Dumplings

Servings: 2
Cooking Time:xx

Ingredients:
- 14 frozen dumplings (pierogies)
- 1 onion
- 1 tbsp olive oil
- 1 tsp sugar

Directions:
1. Take a large saucepan and fill with water, bringing to the boil
2. Cook the dumplings for 5 minutes, remove and drain
3. Slice the onion into long pieces
4. Oil the air fryer basket and preheat to 220ºC
5. Cook the onion for 12 minutes, stirring often. After 5 minutes, add the sugar and combine
6. Remove the onions and place to one side
7. Add the dumplings to the air fryer and cook for 4 minutes
8. Turn the temperature up to 270ºC and cook for another 3 minutes
9. Mix the dumplings with the onions before serving

Vegan Fried Ravioli

Servings: 4
Cooking Time:xx

Ingredients:
- 100g panko breadcrumbs
- 2 tsp yeast
- 1 tsp basil
- 1 tsp oregano
- 1 tsp garlic powder
- Pinch salt and pepper
- 50ml liquid from can of chickpeas
- 150g vegan ravioli
- Cooking spray
- 50g marinara for dipping

Directions:
1. Combine the breadcrumbs, yeast, basil, oregano, garlic powder and salt and pepper
2. Put the liquid from the chickpeas in a bowl
3. Dip the ravioli in the liquid then dip into the breadcrumb mix
4. Heat the air fryer to 190ºC
5. Place the ravioli in the air fryer and cook for about 6 minutes until crispy

Shakshuka

Servings: 2
Cooking Time:xx

Ingredients:
- 2 eggs
- BASE
- 100 g/3½ oz. thinly sliced (bell) peppers
- 1 red onion, halved and thinly sliced
- 2 medium tomatoes, chopped
- 2 teaspoons olive oil
- ¼ teaspoon salt
- ¼ teaspoon freshly ground black pepper
- ½ teaspoon chilli/hot red pepper flakes
- SAUCE
- 100 g/3½ oz. passata/strained tomatoes
- 1 tablespoon tomato purée/paste
- 1 teaspoon balsamic vinegar
- ½ teaspoon runny honey
- ½ teaspoon ground cumin
- ½ teaspoon paprika
- ¼ teaspoon salt
- ⅛ teaspoon freshly ground black pepper

Directions:
1. Preheat the air-fryer to 180°C/350°F.
2. Combine the base ingredients together in a baking dish that fits inside your air-fryer. Add the dish to the preheated air-fryer and air-fry for 10 minutes, stirring halfway through cooking.
3. Meanwhile, combine the sauce ingredients in a bowl. Pour this into the baking dish when the 10 minutes are up. Stir, then make a couple of wells in the sauce for the eggs. Crack the eggs into the wells, then cook for a further 5 minutes or until the eggs are just cooked and yolks still runny. Remove from the air-fryer and serve.

Courgette Meatballs

Servings: 4
Cooking Time:xx

Ingredients:
- 400g oats
- 40g feta, crumbled
- 1 beaten egg
- Salt and pepper
- 150g courgette
- 1 tsp lemon rind
- 6 basil leaves, thinly sliced
- 1 tsp dill

- 1 tsp oregano

Directions:
1. Preheat the air fryer to 200ºC
2. Grate the courgette into a bowl, squeeze any access water out
3. Add all the remaining ingredients apart from the oats and mix well
4. Blend the oats until they resemble breadcrumbs
5. Add the oats into the other mix and stir well
6. Form into balls and place in the air fryer cook for 10 minutes

Vegan Meatballs

Servings:4
Cooking Time:15 Minutes

Ingredients:
- 2 tbsp olive oil
- 2 tbsp soy sauce
- 1 onion, finely sliced
- 1 large carrot, peeled and grated
- 1 x 400 g / 14 oz can chickpeas, drained and rinsed
- 50 g / 1.8 oz plain flour
- 50 g / 1.8 oz rolled oats
- 2 tbsp roasted cashews, chopped
- 1 tsp garlic powder
- ½ tsp cumin

Directions:
1. Preheat the air fryer to 175 °C / 350 °F and line the air fryer with parchment paper or grease it with olive oil.
2. In a large mixing bowl, combine the olive oil and soy sauce. Add the onion slices and grated carrot and toss to coat in the sauce.
3. Place the vegetables in the air fryer and cook for 5 minutes until slightly soft.
4. Meanwhile, place the chickpeas, plain flour, rolled oats, and roasted cashews in a blender, and mix until well combined
5. Remove the mixture from the blender and stir in the garlic powder and cumin. Add the onions and carrots to the bowl and mix well.
6. Scoop the mixture into small meatballs and place them into the air fryer. Increase the temperature on the machine up to 190 °C / 370 °F and cook the meatballs for 10-12 minutes until golden and crispy.

Chickpea And Sweetcorn Falafel

Servings:4
Cooking Time:15 Minutes

Ingredients:

- ½ onion, sliced
- 2 cloves garlic, peeled and sliced
- 2 tbsp fresh parsley, chopped
- 2 tbsp fresh coriander, chopped
- 2 x 400 g / 14 oz chickpeas, drained and rinsed
- 1 tsp salt
- 1 tsp black pepper
- 1 tsp baking powder
- 1 tsp dried mixed herbs
- 1 tsp cumin
- 1 tsp chili powder
- 50 g / 1.8 oz sweetcorn, fresh or frozen

Directions:

1. Preheat the air fryer to 180 °C / 350 °F and line the bottom of the basket with parchment paper.

2. In a food processor, place the onion, garlic cloves, fresh parsley, and fresh coriander. Pulse the ingredients in 30-second intervals until they form a smooth mixture. Scrape the mixture from the sides of the food processor in between each interval if necessary.

3. Mix in the chickpeas, salt, black pepper, baking powder, dried mixed herbs, cumin, and chili powder. Pulse the mixture until fully combined and smooth. Add more water if the mixture is looking a bit dry. The mixture should be dry but not crumbly.

4. Use a spoon to scoop out 2 tbsp of the chickpea mixture at a time and roll into small, even falafels.

5. Transfer the falafels into the prepared air fryer basket and cook for 12-15 minutes.

6. Serve the falafels either hot or cold as a side dish to your main meal or as part of a large salad.

Tofu Bowls

Servings: 4
Cooking Time:xx

Ingredients:

- 1 block of tofu, cut into cubes
- 40ml soy sauce
- 2 tbsp sesame oil
- 1 tsp garlic powder
- 1 chopped onion
- 2 tbsp Tahini dressing
- 3 bunches baby bok choy, chopped
- 300g quinoa
- 1 medium cucumber, sliced
- 1 cup shredded carrot
- 1 avocado, sliced

Directions:

1. Mix the soy sauce, 1 tbsp sesame oil and garlic powder in a bowl. Add the tofu marinade for 10 minutes

2. Place in the air fryer and cook at 200ºC for 20 minutes turning halfway

3. Heat the remaining sesame oil in a pan and cook the onions for about 4 minutes

4. Add the bok choy and cook for another 4 minutes

5. Divide the quinoa between your bowls add bok choy, carrot, cucumber and avocado. Top with the tofu and drizzle with Tahini

Roasted Cauliflower

Servings: 2
Cooking Time:xx

Ingredients:

- 3 cloves garlic
- 1 tbsp peanut oil
- ½ tsp salt
- ½ tsp paprika
- 400g cauliflower florets

Directions:

1. Preheat air fryer to 200ºC

2. Crush the garlic, place all ingredients in a bowl and mix well

3. Place in the air fryer and cook for about 15 minutes, shaking every 5 minutes

Air-fried Artichoke Hearts

Servings: 7
Cooking Time:xx

Ingredients:

- 14 artichoke hearts
- 200g flour
- ¼ tsp baking powder
- Salt
- 6 tbsp water
- 6 tbsp breadcrumbs
- ¼ tsp basil
- ¼ tsp oregano
- ¼ tsp garlic powder
- ¼ tsp paprika

Directions:

1. Mix the baking powder, salt, flour and water in a bowl
2. In another bowl combine the breadcrumbs and seasonings
3. Dip the artichoke in the batter then coat in breadcrumbs
4. Place in the air fryer and cook at 180ºC for 8 minutes

Tempura Veggies

Servings: 4
Cooking Time:xx

Ingredients:

- 150g flour
- ½ tsp salt
- ½ tsp pepper
- 2 eggs
- 2 tbsp cup water
- 100g avocado wedges
- 100g courgette slices
- 100g panko breadcrumbs
- 2 tsp oil
- 100g green beans
- 100g asparagus spears
- 100g red onion rings
- 100g pepper rings

Directions:

1. Mix together flour, salt and pepper. In another bowl mix eggs and water
2. Stir together panko crumbs and oil in a separate bowl
3. Dip vegetables in the flour mix, then egg and then the bread crumbs
4. Preheat the air fryer to 200ºC
5. Place in the air fryer and cook for about 10 minutes until golden brown

Ratatouille

Servings: 4
Cooking Time:xx

Ingredients:

- ½ small aubergine, cubed
- 1 courgette, cubed
- 1 tomato, cubed
- 1 pepper, cut into cubes
- ½ onion, diced
- 1 fresh cayenne pepper, sliced
- 1 tsp vinegar
- 5 sprigs basil, chopped
- 2 sprigs oregano, chopped
- 1 clove garlic, crushed
- Salt and pepper
- 1 tbsp olive oil
- 1 tbsp white wine

Directions:

1. Preheat air fryer to 200ºC
2. Place all ingredients in a bowl and mix
3. Pour into a baking dish
4. Add dish to the air fryer and cook for 8 minutes, stir then cook for another 10 minutes

Air Fryer Cheese Sandwich

Servings:2
Cooking Time:10 Minutes

Ingredients:

- 4 slices white or wholemeal bread
- 2 tbsp butter
- 50 g / 3.5 oz cheddar cheese, grated

Directions:

1. Preheat the air fryer to 180 °C / 350 °F and line the bottom of the basket with parchment paper.
2. Lay the slices of bread out on a clean surface and butter one side of each. Evenly sprinkle the cheese on two of the slices and cover with the final two slices.
3. Transfer the sandwiches to the air fryer, close the lid, and cook for 5 minutes until the bread is crispy and golden, and the cheese is melted.

Sweet Potato Taquitos

Servings: 10
Cooking Time:xx

Ingredients:
- 1 sweet potato cut into ½ inch pieces
- 1 ½ tsp oil
- 1 chopped onion
- 1 tsp minced garlic
- 400g black beans
- 3 tbsp water
- 10 corn tortillas
- 1 chipotle pepper, chopped
- ½ tsp cumin
- ½ tsp paprika
- ½ chilli powder
- ⅛ tsp salt
- ½ tsp maple syrup

Directions:
1. Place the sweet potato in the air fryer spray with oil and cook for 12 minutes at 200ºC
2. Heat oil in a pan, add the onion and garlic and cook for a few minutes until soft
3. Add remaining ingredients to the pan, add 2 tbsp of water and combine
4. Add the sweet potato and 1 tbsp of water and mix
5. Warm the tortilla in the microwave for about 1 minute
6. Place a row of filling across the centre of each tortilla. Fold up the bottom of the tortilla, tuck under the filling, fold in the edges then continue to roll the tortilla
7. Place in the air fryer and cook for about 12 minutes

Veggie Bakes

Servings: 2
Cooking Time:xx

Ingredients:
- Any type of leftover vegetable bake you have
- 30g flour

Directions:
1. Preheat the air fryer to 180ºC
2. Mix the flour with the leftover vegetable bake
3. Shape into balls and place in the air fryer
4. Cook for 10 minutes

Baked Feta, Tomato & Garlic Pasta

Servings: 2
Cooking Time:xx

Ingredients:
- 100 g/3½ oz. feta or plant-based feta, cubed
- 20 cherry tomatoes
- 2 garlic cloves, peeled and halved
- ¾ teaspoon oregano
- 1 teaspoon chilli/hot red pepper flakes
- ½ teaspoon garlic salt
- 2 tablespoons olive oil
- 100 g/3½ oz. cooked pasta plus about 1 tablespoon of cooking water
- freshly ground black pepper

Directions:
1. Preheat the air-fryer to 200ºC/400ºF.
2. Place the feta, tomatoes and garlic in a baking dish that fits inside your air-fryer. Top with the oregano, chilli/hot red pepper flakes, garlic salt and olive oil. Place the dish in the preheated air-fryer and air-fry for 10 minutes, then remove and stir in the pasta and cooking water. Serve sprinkled with black pepper.

Spicy Spanish Potatoes

Servings: 2
Cooking Time:xx

Ingredients:
- 4 large potatoes
- 1 tbsp olive oil
- 2 tsp paprika
- 2 tsp dried garlic
- 1 tsp barbacoa seasoning
- Salt and pepper

Directions:
1. Chop the potatoes into wedges
2. Place them in a bowl with olive oil and seasoning, mix well
3. Add to the air fryer and cook at 160ºC for 20 minutes
4. Shake, increase heat to 200ºC and cook for another 3 minutes

Lentil Balls With Zingy Rice

Servings: 4
Cooking Time:xx

Ingredients:

- 2 cans lentils
- 200g walnut halves
- 3 tbsp dried mushrooms
- 3 tbsp parsley
- 1 ½ tbsp tomato paste
- ¾ tsp salt
- ½ tsp pepper
- 100g bread crumbs
- 400ml water
- 200g rice
- 2 tbsp lemon juice
- 2 tsp lemon zest
- Salt to taste

Directions:

1. Preheat air fryer to 190°C
2. Place the lentils, walnuts, mushrooms, parsley, tomato paste, salt, pepper in a food processor and blend
3. Fold in the bread crumbs
4. Form the mix into balls and place in the air fryer
5. Cook for 10 minutes turn then cook for a further 5 minutes
6. Add the rice to a pan with water, bring to the boil and simmer for 20 minutes
7. Stir in the lemon juice, lemon zest and salt. Serve

Goat's Cheese Tartlets

Servings: 2
Cooking Time:xx

Ingredients:

- 1 readymade sheet of puff pastry, 35 x 23 cm/14 x 9 in. (gluten-free if you wish)
- 4 tablespoons pesto (jarred or see page 80)
- 4 roasted baby (bell) peppers (see page 120)
- 4 tablespoons soft goat's cheese
- 2 teaspoons milk (plant-based if you wish)

Directions:

1. Cut the pastry sheet in half along the long edge, to make two smaller rectangles. Fold in the edges of each pastry rectangle to form a crust. Using a fork, prick a few holes in the base of the pastry. Brush half the pesto onto each rectangle, top with the peppers and goat's cheese. Brush the pastry crust with milk.
2. Preheat the air-fryer to 180°C/350°F.

3. Place one tartlet on an air-fryer liner or a piece of pierced parchment paper in the preheated air-fryer and air-fry for 6 minutes (you'll need to cook them one at a time). Repeat with the second tartlet.

Falafel Burgers

Servings: 2
Cooking Time:xx

Ingredients:

- 1 large can of chickpeas
- 1 onion
- 1 lemon
- 140g oats
- 28g grated cheese
- 28g feta cheese
- Salt and pepper to taste
- 3 tbsp Greek yogurt
- 4 tbsp soft cheese
- 1 tbsp garlic puree
- 1 tbsp coriander
- 1 tbsp oregano
- 1 tbsp parsley

Directions:

1. Place the chickpeas, onion, lemon rind, garlic and seasonings and blend until coarse
2. Add the mix to a bowl and stir in half the soft cheese, cheese and feta
3. Form in to burger shape and coat in the oats
4. Place in the air fryer and cook at 180°C for 8 minutes
5. To make the sauce mix the remaining soft cheese, greek yogurt and lemon juice in a bowl

Artichoke Pasta

Servings: 2
Cooking Time:xx

Ingredients:
- 100g pasta
- 50g basil leaves
- 6 artichoke hearts
- 2 tbsp pumpkin seeds
- 2 tbsp lemon juice
- 1 clove garlic
- ½ tsp white miso paste
- 1 can chickpeas
- 1 tsp olive oil

Directions:
1. Place the chickpeas in the air fryer and cook at 200ºC for 12 minutes
2. Cook the pasta according to packet instructions
3. Add the remaining ingredients to a food processor and blend
4. Add the pasta to a bowl and spoon over the pesto mix
5. Serve and top with roasted chickpeas

Radish Hash Browns

Servings: 4
Cooking Time:xx

Ingredients:
- 300g radish
- 1 onion
- 1 tsp onion powder
- ¾ tsp sea salt
- ½ tsp paprika
- ¼ tsp ground black pepper
- 1 tsp coconut oil

Directions:
1. Wash the radish, trim off the roots and slice in a processor along with the onions
2. Add the coconut oil and mix well
3. Put the onions and radish into the air fryer and cook at 180ºC for 8 minutes shaking a few times
4. Put the onion and radish in a bowl add seasoning and mix well
5. Put back in the air fryer and cook at 200ºC for 5 minutes

Miso Mushrooms On Sourdough Toast

Servings: 1
Cooking Time:xx

Ingredients:
- 1 teaspoon miso paste
- 1 teaspoon oil, such as avocado or coconut (melted)
- 1 teaspoon soy sauce
- 80 g/3 oz. chestnut mushrooms, sliced 5 mm/½ in. thick
- 1 large slice sourdough bread
- 2 teaspoons butter or plant-based spread
- a little freshly chopped flat-leaf parsley, to serve

Directions:
1. Preheat the air-fryer to 200ºC/400ºF.
2. In a small bowl or ramekin mix together the miso paste, oil and soy sauce.
3. Place the mushrooms in a small shallow gratin dish that fits inside your air-fryer. Add the sauce to the mushrooms and mix together. Place the gratin dish in the preheated air-fryer and air-fry for 6–7 minutes, stirring once during cooking.
4. With 4 minutes left to cook, add the bread to the air-fryer and turn over at 2 minutes whilst giving the mushrooms a final stir.
5. Once cooked, butter the toast and serve the mushrooms on top, scattered with chopped parsley.

Whole Wheat Pizza

Servings: 2
Cooking Time:xx

Ingredients:
- 100g marinara sauce
- 2 whole wheat pitta
- 200g baby spinach leaves
- 1 small plum tomato, sliced
- 1 clove garlic, sliced
- 400g grated cheese
- 50g shaved parmesan

Directions:
1. Preheat air fryer to 160ºC
2. Spread each of the pitta with marinara sauce
3. Sprinkle with cheese, top with spinach, plum tomato and garlic. Finish with parmesan shavings
4. Place in the air fryer and cook for about 4 mins cheese has melted

Spanakopita Bites

Servings: 4
Cooking Time:xx

Ingredients:
- 300g baby spinach
- 2 tbsp water
- 100g cottage cheese
- 50g feta cheese
- 2 tbsp grated parmesan
- 1 tbsp olive oil
- 4 sheets of filo pastry
- 1 large egg white
- 1 tsp lemon zest
- 1 tsp oregano
- ¼ tsp salt
- ¼ tsp pepper
- ⅛ tsp cayenne

Directions:
1. Place spinach in water and cook for about 5 minutes, drain
2. Mix all ingredients together
3. Place a sheet of pastry down and brush with oil, place another on the top and do the same, continue until all four on top of each other
4. Ut the pastry into 8 strips then cut each strip in half across the middle
5. Add 1 tbsp of mix to each piece of pastry
6. Fold one corner over the mix to create a triangle, fold over the other corner to seal
7. Place in the air fryer and cook at 190ºC for about 12 minutes until golden brown

Buffalo Cauliflower Bites

Servings: 4
Cooking Time:xx

Ingredients:
- 3 tbsp ketchup
- 2 tbsp hot sauce
- 1 large egg white
- 200g panko bread crumbs
- 400g cauliflower
- ¼ tsp black pepper
- Cooking spray
- 40g sour cream
- 40g blue cheese
- 1 garlic clove, grated
- 1 tsp red wine vinegar

Directions:
1. Whisk together ketchup, hot sauce and egg white
2. Place the breadcrumbs in another bowl
3. Dip the cauliflower in the sauce then in the breadcrumbs
4. Coat with cooking spray
5. Place in the air fryer and cook at 160ºC for about 20 minutes until crispy
6. Mix remaining ingredients together and serve as a dip

Jackfruit Taquitos

Servings: 2
Cooking Time:xx

Ingredients:
- 1 large Jackfruit
- 250g red beans
- 100g pico de gallo sauce
- 50ml water
- 2 tbsp water
- 4 wheat tortillas
- Olive oil spray

Directions:
1. Place the jackfruit, red beans, sauce and water in a saucepan
2. Bring to the boil and simmer for 25 minutes
3. Preheat the air fryer to 185ºC
4. Mash the jackfruit mixture, add ¼ cup of the mix to each tortilla and roll up tightly
5. Spray with olive oil and place in the air fryer
6. Cook for 8 minutes

Side Dishes Recipes

Side Dishes Recipes

Sweet Potato Tots

Servings: 24
Cooking Time:xx

Ingredients:
- 2 sweet potatoes, peeled
- ½ tsp cajun seasoning
- Olive oil cooking spray
- Sea salt to taste

Directions:
1. Boil the sweet potatoes in a pan for about 15 minutes, allow to cool
2. Grate the sweet potato and mix in the cajun seasoning
3. Form into tot shaped cylinders
4. Spray the air fryer with oil, place the tots in the air fryer
5. Sprinkle with salt and cook for 8 minutes at 200ºC, turn and cook for another 8 minutes

Aubergine Parmesan

Servings: 4
Cooking Time:xx

Ingredients:
- 100g Italian breadcrumbs
- 50g grated parmesan
- 1 tsp Italian seasoning
- 1 tsp salt
- ½ tsp dried basil
- ½ tsp onion powder
- ½ tsp black pepper
- 100g flour
- 2 eggs
- 1 aubergine, sliced into ½ inch rounds

Directions:
1. Mix breadcrumbs, parmesan, salt Italian seasoning, basil, onion powder and pepper in a bowl
2. Add the flour to another bowl, and beat the eggs in another
3. Dip the aubergine in the flour, then the eggs and then coat in the bread crumbs
4. Preheat the air fryer to 185ºC
5. Place the aubergine in the air fryer and cook for 8-10 minutes
6. Turnover and cook for a further 4-6 minutes

Egg Fried Rice

Servings:2
Cooking Time:15 Minutes

Ingredients:
- 400 g / 14 oz cooked white or brown rice
- 100 g / 3.5 oz fresh peas and sweetcorn
- 2 tbsp olive oil
- 2 eggs, scrambled

Directions:
1. Preheat the air fryer to 150 °C / 300 °F and line the bottom of the basket with parchment paper.
2. In a bowl, mix the cooked white or brown rice and the fresh peas and sweetcorn.
3. Pour in 2 tbsp olive oil and toss to coat evenly. Stir in the scrambled eggs.
4. Transfer the egg rice into the lined air fryer basket, close the lid, and cook for 15 minutes until the eggs are cooked and the rice is soft.
5. Serve as a side dish with some cooked meat or tofu.

Butternut Squash

Servings: 4
Cooking Time:xx

Ingredients:
- 500 g/1 lb. 2 oz. butternut squash, chopped into 2.5-cm/1-in. cubes
- 1 tablespoon olive oil or avocado oil
- 1 teaspoon smoked paprika
- 1 teaspoon dried oregano
- ½ teaspoon salt
- ¼ teaspoon freshly ground black pepper

Directions:
1. Preheat the air-fryer to 180ºC/350ºF
2. In a bowl toss the butternut squash cubes in the oil and all the seasonings.
3. Add the butternut squash cubes to the preheated air-fryer and air-fry for 16–18 minutes, shaking the drawer once during cooking.

Super Easy Fries

Servings: 2
Cooking Time:xx

Ingredients:
- 500g potatoes cut into ½ inch sticks
- 1 tsp olive oil
- ¼ tsp salt
- ¼ tsp pepper

Directions:
1. Place the potatoes in a bowl cover with water and allow to soak for 30 minutes
2. Spread the butter onto one side of the bread slices
3. Pat dry with paper, drizzle with oil and toss to coat
4. Place in the air fryer and cook at 200°C for about 15 minutes, keep tossing through cooking time
5. Sprinkle with salt and pepper

Carrot & Parmesan Chips

Servings: 2
Cooking Time:xx

Ingredients:
- 180g carrots
- 1 tbsp olive oil
- 2 tbsp grated parmesan
- 1 crushed garlic clove
- Salt and pepper for seasoning

Directions:
1. Take a mixing bowl and add the olive oil and garlic, combining well
2. Remove the tops of the carrots and cut into halves, and then another half
3. Add the carrots to the bowl and toss well
4. Add the parmesan and coat the carrots well
5. Add the carrots to the air fryer and cook for 20 minutes at 220°C, shaking halfway through

Alternative Stuffed Potatoes

Servings: 4
Cooking Time:xx

Ingredients:
- 4 baking potatoes, peeled and halved
- 1 tbsp olive oil
- 150g grated cheese
- ½ onion, diced
- 2 slices bacon

Directions:
1. Preheat air fryer to 175°C
2. Brush the potatoes with oil and cook in the air fryer for 10 minutes
3. Coat again with oil and cook for a further 10 minutes
4. Cut the potatoes in half spoon the insides into a bowl and mix in the cheese
5. Place the bacon and onion in a pan and cook until browned, mix in with the potato
6. Stuff the skins with the mix and return to the air fryer, cook for about 6 minutes

Zingy Brussels Sprouts

Servings: 2
Cooking Time:xx

Ingredients:
- 1 tbsp avocado oil
- ½ tsp salt
- ½ tsp pepper
- 400g Brussels sprouts halved
- 1 tsp balsamic vinegar
- 2 tsp crumbled bacon

Directions:
1. Preheat air fryer to 175°C
2. Combine oil, salt and pepper in a bowl and mix well. Add Brussels sprouts
3. Place in the air fryer and cook for 5 minutes shake then cook for another 5 minutes
4. Sprinkle with balsamic vinegar and sprinkle with bacon

Mediterranean Vegetables

Servings: 1–2
Cooking Time:xx

Ingredients:

- 1 courgette/zucchini, thickly sliced
- 1 (bell) pepper, deseeded and chopped into large chunks
- 1 red onion, sliced into wedges
- 12 cherry tomatoes
- 1 tablespoon olive oil
- ½ teaspoon salt
- ½ teaspoon freshly ground black pepper
- 2 rosemary twigs
- mozzarella, fresh pesto (see page 80) and basil leaves, to serve

Directions:

1. Preheat the air-fryer to 180ºC/350ºF.
2. Toss the prepared vegetables in the oil and seasoning. Add the vegetables and the rosemary to the preheated air-fryer and air-fry for 12–14 minutes, depending on how 'chargrilled' you like them.
3. Remove and serve topped with fresh mozzarella and pesto and scattered with basil leaves.

Orange Tofu

Servings: 4
Cooking Time:xx

Ingredients:

- 400g tofu, drained
- 1 tbsp tamari
- 1 tbsp corn starch
- ¼ tsp pepper flakes
- 1 tsp minced ginger
- 1 tsp fresh garlic
- 1 tsp orange zest
- 75ml orange juice
- 75ml water
- 2 tsp cornstarch
- 1 tbsp maple syrup

Directions:

1. Cut the tofu into cubes, place in a bowl add the tamari and mix well
2. Mix in 1 tbsp starch and allow to marinate for 30 minutes
3. Place the remaining ingredients into another bowl and mix well
4. Place the tofu in the air fryer and cook at 190ºC for about 10 minutes
5. Add tofu to a pan with sauce mix and cook until sauce thickens

Corn On The Cob

Servings: 4
Cooking Time:xx

Ingredients:

- 75g mayo
- 2 tsp grated cheese
- 1 tsp lime juice
- ¼ tsp chilli powder
- 2 ears of corn, cut into 4

Directions:

1. Heat the air fryer to 200ºC
2. Mix the mayo, cheese lime juice and chilli powder in a bowl
3. Cover the corn in the mayo mix
4. Place in the air fryer and cook for 8 minutes

Tex Mex Hash Browns

Servings: 4
Cooking Time:xx

Ingredients:

- 500g potatoes cut into cubes
- 1 tbsp olive oil
- 1 red pepper
- 1 onion
- 1 jalapeño pepper
- ½ tsp taco seasoning
- ½ tsp cumin
- Salt and pepper to taste

Directions:

1. Soak the potatoes in water for 20 minutes
2. Heat the air fryer to 160ºC
3. Drain the potatoes and coat with olive oil
4. Add to the air fryer and cook for 18 minutes
5. Mix the remaining ingredients in a bowl, add the potatoes and mix well
6. Place the mix into the air fryer cook for 6 minutes, shake and cook for a further 5 minutes

Mexican Rice

Servings: 4
Cooking Time:xx

Ingredients:
- 500g long grain rice
- 3 tbsp olive oil
- 60ml water
- 1 tsp chilli powder
- 1/4 tsp cumin
- 2 tbsp tomato paste
- 1/2 tsp garlic powder
- 1tsp red pepper flakes
- 1 chopped onion
- 500ml chicken stock
- Half a small jalapeño pepper with seeds out, chopped
- Salt for seasoning

Directions:
1. Add the water and tomato paste and combine, placing to one side
2. Take a baking pan and add a little oil
3. Wash the rice and add to the baking pan
4. Add the chicken stock, tomato paste, jalapeños, onions, and the rest of the olive oil, and combine
5. Place aluminium foil over the top and place in your air fryer
6. Cook at 220ºC for 50 minutes
7. Keep checking the rice as it cooks, as the liquid should be absorbing

Orange Sesame Cauliflower

Servings: 4
Cooking Time:xx

Ingredients:
- 100ml water
- 30g cornstarch
- 50g flour
- 1/2 tsp salt
- ½ tsp pepper
- 2 tbsp tomato ketchup
- 2 tbsp brown sugar
- 1 sliced onion

Directions:
1. Mix together flour, cornstarch, water, salt and pepper until smooth
2. Coat the cauliflower and chill for 30 minutes
3. Place in the air fryer and cook for 22 minutes at

170ºC
4. Meanwhile combine remaining ingredients in a saucepan, gently simmer until thickened.
5. Mix cauliflower with sauce and top with toasted sesame seeds to serve

Cauliflower With Hot Sauce And Blue Cheese Sauce

Servings:2
Cooking Time:15 Minutes

Ingredients:
- For the cauliflower:
- 1 cauliflower, broken into florets
- 4 tbsp hot sauce
- 2 tbsp olive oil
- 1 tsp garlic powder
- ½ tsp salt
- ½ tsp black pepper
- 1 tbsp plain flour
- 1 tbsp corn starch
- For the blue cheese sauce:
- 50 g / 1.8 oz blue cheese, crumbled
- 2 tbsp sour cream
- 2 tbsp mayonnaise
- ½ tsp salt
- ½ tsp black pepper

Directions:
1. Preheat the air fryer to 180 °C / 350 °F and line the bottom of the basket with parchment paper.
2. In a bowl, combine the hot sauce, olive oil, garlic powder, salt, and black pepper until it forms a consistent mixture. Add the cauliflower to the bowl and coat in the sauce.
3. Stir in the plain flour and corn starch until well combined.
4. Transfer the cauliflower to the lined basket in the air fryer, close the lid, and cook for 12-15 minutes until the cauliflower has softened and is golden in colour.
5. Meanwhile, make the blue cheese sauce by combining all of the ingredients. When the cauliflower is ready, remove it from the air fryer and serve with the blue cheese sauce on the side.

Air Fryer Eggy Bread

Servings:2
Cooking Time:5-7 Minutes

Ingredients:
- 4 slices white bread
- 4 eggs, beaten
- 1 tsp black pepper
- 1 tsp dried chives

Directions:
1. Preheat your air fryer to 150 °C / 300 °F and line the bottom of the basket with parchment paper.
2. Whisk the eggs in a large mixing bowl and soak each slice of bread until fully coated.
3. Transfer the eggy bread to the preheated air fryer and cook for 5-7 minutes until the eggs are set and the bread is crispy.
4. Serve hot with a sprinkle of black pepper and chives on top.

Grilled Bacon And Cheese

Servings: 2
Cooking Time:xx

Ingredients:
- 4 slices of regular bread
- 1 tbsp butter
- 2 slices cheddar cheese
- 5 slices bacon, pre-cooked
- 2 slices mozzarella cheese

Directions:
1. Place the butter into the microwave to melt
2. Spread the butter onto one side of the bread slices
3. Place one slice of bread into the fryer basket, with the buttered side facing downwards
4. Place the cheddar on top, followed by the bacon, mozzarella and the other slice of bread, with the buttered side facing upwards
5. Set your fryer to 170ºC and cook the sandwich for 4 minutes
6. Turn the sandwich over and cook for another 3 minutes
7. Turn the sandwich out and serve whilst hot
8. Repeat with the other remaining sandwich

Potato Hay

Servings: 4
Cooking Time:xx

Ingredients:
- 2 potatoes
- 1 tbsp oil
- Salt and pepper to taste

Directions:
1. Cut the potatoes into spirals
2. Soak in a bowl of water for 20 minutes, drain and pat dry
3. Add oil, salt and pepper and mix well to coat
4. Preheat air fryer to 180ºC
5. Add potatoes to air fryer and cook for 5 minutes, toss then cook for another 12 until golden brown

Zingy Roasted Carrots

Servings: 4
Cooking Time:xx

Ingredients:
- 500g carrots
- 1 tsp olive oil
- 1 tsp cayenne pepper
- Salt and pepper for seasoning

Directions:
1. Peel the carrots and cut them into chunks, around 2" in size
2. Preheat your air fryer to 220ºC
3. Add the carrots to a bowl with the olive oil and cayenne and toss to coat
4. Place in the fryer and cook for 15 minutes, giving them a stir halfway through
5. Season before serving

Potato Wedges With Rosemary

Servings: 2
Cooking Time:xx

Ingredients:

- 2 potatoes, sliced into wedges
- 1 tbsp olive oil
- 2 tsp seasoned salt
- 2 tbsp chopped rosemary

Directions:

1. Preheat air fryer to 190ºC
2. Drizzle potatoes with oil, mix in salt and rosemary
3. Place in the air fryer and cook for 20 minutes turning halfway

Roasted Okra

Servings: 1
Cooking Time:xx

Ingredients:

- 300g Okra, ends trimmed and pods sliced
- 1 tsp olive oil
- ¼ tsp salt
- ⅛ tsp pepper

Directions:

1. Preheat the air fryer to 175ºC
2. Combine all ingredients in a bowl and stir gently
3. Place in the air fryer and cook for 5 minutes, shake and cook for another 5 minutes

Sweet And Sticky Parsnips And Carrots

Servings:2
Cooking Time:15 Minutes

Ingredients:

- 4 large carrots, peeled and chopped into long chunks
- 4 large parsnips, peeled and chopped into long chunks
- 1 tbsp olive oil
- 2 tbsp honey
- 1 tsp dried mixed herbs

Directions:

1. Preheat the air fryer to 150 °C / 300 °F and line the bottom of the basket with parchment paper.
2. Place the chopped carrots and parsnips in a large bowl and drizzle over the olive oil and honey. Sprinkle in some black pepper to taste and toss well to fully coat the vegetables.

3. Transfer the coated vegetables into the air fryer basket and shut the lid. Cook for 20 minutes until the carrots and parsnips and cooked and crispy.
4. Serve as a side with your dinner.

Cheesy Garlic Asparagus

Servings: 4
Cooking Time:xx

Ingredients:

- 1 tsp olive oil
- 500g asparagus
- 1 tsp garlic salt
- 1 tbsp grated parmesan cheese
- Salt and pepper for seasoning

Directions:

1. Preheat the air fryer to 270ºC
2. Clean the asparagus and cut off the bottom 1"
3. Pat dry and place in the air fryer, covering with the oil
4. Sprinkle the parmesan and garlic salt on top, seasoning to your liking
5. Cook for between 7 and 10 minutes
6. Add a little extra parmesan over the top before serving

Air Fryer Corn On The Cob

Servings: 2
Cooking Time:xx

Ingredients:

- 2 corn on the cob
- 2 tbsp melted butter
- A pinch of salt
- 1/2 tsp dried parsley
- 2 tbsp grated parmesan

Directions:

1. Preheat the air fryer to 270ºC
2. Take a bowl and combine the melted butter, salt and parsley
3. Brush the corn with the mixture
4. Add the corn inside the air fryer and cook for 14 minutes
5. Remove the corn from the fryer and roll in the grated cheese

Cheesy Broccoli

Servings:4
Cooking Time:5 Minutes

Ingredients:
- 1 large broccoli head, broken into florets
- 4 tbsp soft cheese
- 1 tsp black pepper
- 50 g / 3.5 oz cheddar cheese, grated

Directions:
1. Preheat the air fryer to 150 °C / 300 °F and line the mesh basket with parchment paper or grease it with olive oil.
2. Wash and drain the broccoli florets and place in a bowl and stir in the soft cheese and black pepper to fully coat all of the florets.
3. Transfer the broccoli to the air fryer basket and sprinkle the cheddar cheese on top. Close the lid and cook for 5-7 minutes until the broccoli has softened and the cheese has melted.
4. Serve as a side dish to your favourite meal.

Honey Roasted Parsnips

Servings: 4
Cooking Time:xx

Ingredients:
- 350 g/12 oz. parsnips
- 1 tablespoon plain/all-purpose flour (gluten-free if you wish)
- 1½ tablespoons runny honey
- 2 tablespoons olive oil
- salt

Directions:
1. Top and tail the parsnips, then slice lengthways, about 2 cm/¾ in. wide. Place in a saucepan with water to cover and a good pinch of salt. Bring to the boil, then boil for 5 minutes.
2. Remove and drain well, allowing any excess water to evaporate. Dust the parsnips with flour. Mix together the honey and oil in a small bowl, then toss in the parsnips to coat well in the honey and oil.
3. Preheat the air-fryer to 180°C/350°F.
4. Add the parsnips to the preheated air-fryer and air-fry for 14–16 minutes, depending on how dark you like the outsides (the longer you cook them, the sweeter they get).

Sweet Potato Wedges

Servings:4
Cooking Time:20 Minutes

Ingredients:
- ½ tsp garlic powder
- ½ tsp cumin
- ½ tsp smoked paprika
- ½ tsp cayenne pepper
- ½ tsp salt
- ½ tsp black pepper
- 1 tsp dried chives
- 4 tbsp olive oil
- 3 large sweet potatoes, cut into wedges

Directions:
1. Preheat the air fryer to 180 °C / 350 °F and line the bottom of the basket with parchment paper.
2. In a bowl, mix the garlic powder, cumin, smoked paprika, cayenne pepper, salt, black pepper, and dried chives until combined.
3. Whisk in the olive oil and coat the sweet potato wedges in the spicy oil mixture.
4. Transfer the coated sweet potatoes to the air fryer and close the lid. Cook for 20 minutes until cooked and crispy. Serve hot as a side with your main meal.

Garlic And Parsley Potatoes

Servings: 4
Cooking Time:xx

Ingredients:
- 500g baby potatoes, cut into quarters
- 1 tbsp oil
- 1 tsp salt
- ½ tsp garlic powder
- ½ tsp dried parsley

Directions:
1. Preheat air fryer to 175ºC
2. Combine potatoes and oil in a bowl
3. Add remaining ingredients and mix
4. Add to the air fryer and cook for about 25 minutes until golden brown, turning halfway through

Crispy Cinnamon French Toast

Servings:2
Cooking Time:5 Minutes

Ingredients:
- 4 slices white bread
- 4 eggs
- 200 ml milk (cow's milk, cashew milk, soy milk, or oat milk)
- 2 tbsp granulated sugar
- 1 tsp brown sugar
- 1 tsp vanilla extract
- ½ tsp ground cinnamon

Directions:
1. Preheat your air fryer to 150 °C / 300 °F and line the bottom of the basket with parchment paper.
2. Cut each of the bread slices into 2 even rectangles and set them aside.
3. In a mixing bowl, whisk together the 4 eggs, milk, granulated sugar, brown sugar, vanilla extract, and ground cinnamon.
4. Soak the bread pieces in the egg mixture until they are fully covered and soaked in the mixture.
5. Place the coated bread slices in the lined air fryer, close the lid, and cook for 4-5 minutes until the bread is crispy and golden.
6. Serve the French toast slices with whatever toppings you desire.

Sweet & Spicy Baby Peppers

Servings: 2
Cooking Time:xx

Ingredients:
- 200 g/7 oz. piccarella (baby) peppers, deseeded and quartered lengthways
- 1 teaspoon olive oil
- ½ teaspoon chilli/chili paste
- ¼ teaspoon runny honey
- salt and freshly ground black pepper

Directions:
1. Preheat the air-fryer to 180ºC/350ºF.
2. Toss the peppers in the oil, chilli/chili paste and honey, then add salt and pepper to taste.
3. Place in the preheated air-fryer and air-fry for 6–8 minutes, depending on how 'chargrilled' you like them, turning them over halfway through.

Ricotta Stuffed Aubergine

Servings: 2
Cooking Time:xx

Ingredients:
- 1 aubergine
- 150g ricotta cheese
- 75g Parmesan cheese, plus an extra 75g for the breading
- 1 tsp garlic powder
- 3 tbsp parsley
- 1 egg, plus an extra 2 eggs for the breading
- 300g pork rind crumbs
- 2 tsp Italian seasoning

Directions:
1. Cut the aubergine into rounds, about 1/2" in thickness
2. Line a baking sheet with parchment and arrange the rounds on top, sprinkling with salt
3. Place another sheet of parchment on top and place something heavy on top to get rid of excess water
4. Leave for 30 minutes
5. Take a bowl and combine the egg, ricotta, 75g Parmesan and parsley, until smooth
6. Remove the parchment from the aubergine and wipe off the salt
7. Take a tablespoon of the ricotta mixture and place on top of each round of aubergine, spreading with a knife
8. Place in the freezer for a while to set
9. Take a bowl and add the two eggs, the pork rinds, parmesan and seasonings, and combine
10. Remove the aubergine from the freezer and coat each one in the mixture completely
11. Place back in the freezer for 45 minutes
12. Cook in the air fryer for 8 minutes at 250ºC

Poultry Recipes

Poultry Recipes

Smoky Chicken Breast

Servings: 2
Cooking Time:xx

Ingredients:
- 2 halved chicken breasts
- 2 tsp olive oil
- 1 tsp ground thyme
- 2 tsp paprika
- 1tsp cumin
- 0.5 tsp cayenne pepper
- 0.5 tsp onion powder
- Salt and pepper to taste

Directions:
1. In a medium bowl, combine the spices together
2. Pour the spice mixture onto a plate
3. Take each chicken breast and coat in the spices, pressing down to ensure an even distribution
4. Place the chicken to one side for 5 minutes
5. Preheat your air fryer to 180°C
6. Arrange the chicken inside the fryer and cook for 10 minutes
7. Turn the chicken over and cook for another 10 minutes
8. Remove from the fryer and allow to sit for 5 minutes before serving

Chicken Tikka Masala

Servings: 4
Cooking Time:xx

Ingredients:
- 100g tikka masala curry pasta
- 200g low fat yogurt
- 600g skinless chicken breasts
- 1 tbsp vegetable oil
- 1 onion, chopped
- 400g can of the whole, peeled tomatoes
- 20ml water
- 1 tbsp sugar
- 2 tbsp lemon juice
- 1 small bunch of chopped coriander leaves

Directions:
1. Take a bowl and combine the tikka masala curry paste with half the yogurt
2. Cut the chicken into strips

3. Preheat the air fryer to 200°C
4. Add the yogurt mixture and coat the chicken until fully covered
5. Place into the refrigerator for 2 hours
6. Place the oil and onion in the air fryer and cook for 10 minutes
7. Add the marinated chicken, tomatoes, water and the rest of the yogurt and combine
8. Add the sugar and lemon juice and combine again
9. Cook for 15 minutes

Sticky Chicken Tikka Drumsticks

Servings: 4
Cooking Time:xx

Ingredients:
- 12 chicken drumsticks
- MARINADE`
- 100 g/½ cup Greek yogurt
- 2 tablespoons tikka paste
- 2 teaspoons ginger preserve
- freshly squeezed juice of ½ a lemon
- ¾ teaspoon salt

Directions:
1. Make slices across each of the drumsticks with a sharp knife. Mix the marinade ingredients together in a bowl, then add the drumsticks. Massage the marinade into the drumsticks, then leave to marinate in the fridge overnight or for at least 6 hours.
2. Preheat the air-fryer to 200°C/400°F.
3. Lay the drumsticks on an air-fryer liner or a piece of pierced parchment paper. Place the paper and drumsticks in the preheated air-fryer. Air-fry for 6 minutes, then turn over and cook for a further 6 minutes. Check the internal temperature of the drumsticks has reached at least 75°C/167°F using a meat thermometer – if not, cook for another few minutes and then serve.

Olive Stained Turkey Breast

Servings: 14
Cooking Time:xx

Ingredients:
- The brine from a can of olives
- 150ml buttermilk
- 300g boneless and skinless turkey breasts
- 1 sprig fresh rosemary
- 2 sprigs fresh thyme

Directions:
1. Take a mixing bowl and combine the olive brine and buttermilk
2. Pour the mixture over the turkey breast
3. Add the rosemary and thyme sprigs
4. Place into the refrigerator for 8 hours
5. Remove from the fridge and let the turkey reach room temperature
6. Preheat the air fryer to 175C
7. Cook for 15 minutes, ensuring the turkey is cooked through before serving

Chicken & Potatoes

Servings: 4
Cooking Time:xx

Ingredients:
- 2 tbsp olive oil
- 2 potatoes, cut into 2" pieces
- 2 chicken breasts, cut into pieces of around 1" size
- 4 crushed garlic cloves
- 2 tsp smoked paprika
- 1 tsp thyme
- 1/2 tsp red chilli flakes
- Salt and pepper to taste

Directions:
1. Preheat your air fryer to 260°C
2. Take a large bowl and combine the potatoes with half of the garlic, half the paprika, half the chilli flakes, salt, pepper and half the oil
3. Place into the air fryer and cook for 5 minutes, before turning over and cooking for another 5 minutes
4. Take a bowl and add the chicken with the rest of the seasonings and oil, until totally coated
5. Add the chicken to the potatoes mixture, moving the potatoes to the side
6. Cook for 10 minutes, turning the chicken halfway through

Chicken And Wheat Stir Fry

Servings: 4
Cooking Time:xx

Ingredients:
- 1 onion
- 1 clove of garlic
- 200g skinless boneless chicken breast halves
- 3 whole tomatoes
- 400ml water
- 1 chicken stock cube
- 1 tbsp curry powder
- 130g wheat berries
- 1 tbsp vegetable oil

Directions:
1. Thinly slice the onion and garlic
2. Chop the chicken and tomatoes into cubes
3. Take a large saucepan and add the water, chicken stock, curry powder and wheat berries, combining well
4. Pour the oil into the air fryer bowl and heat for 5 minutes at 200°C
5. Add the remaining ingredients and pour the contents into the air fryer
6. Cook for 15 minutes

Whole Chicken

Servings: 4
Cooking Time:xx

Ingredients:
- 1.5-kg/3¼-lb. chicken
- 2 tablespoons butter or coconut oil
- salt and freshly ground black pepper

Directions:
1. Place the chicken breast-side up and carefully insert the butter or oil between the skin and the flesh of each breast. Season.
2. Preheat the air-fryer to 180°C/350°F. If the chicken hits the heating element, remove the drawer to lower the chicken a level.
3. Add the chicken to the preheated air-fryer breast-side up. Air-fry for 30 minutes, then turn over and cook for a further 10 minutes. Check the internal temperature with a meat thermometer. If it is 75°C/167°F at the thickest part, remove the chicken from the air-fryer and leave to rest for 10 minutes before carving. If less than 75°C/167°F, continue to cook until this internal temperature is reached and then allow to rest.

Pizza Chicken Nuggets

Servings: 2
Cooking Time:xx

Ingredients:

- 60 g/¾ cup dried breadcrumbs (see page 9)
- 20 g/¼ cup grated Parmesan
- ½ teaspoon dried oregano
- ¼ teaspoon freshly ground black pepper
- 150 g/⅔ cup Mediterranean sauce (see page 102) or 150 g/5½ oz. jarred tomato pasta sauce (keep any left-over sauce for serving)
- 400 g/14 oz. chicken fillets

Directions:

1. Preheat the air-fryer to 180°C/350°F.
2. Combine the breadcrumbs, Parmesan, oregano and pepper in a bowl. Have the Mediterranean or pasta sauce in a separate bowl.
3. Dip each chicken fillet in the tomato sauce first, then roll in the breadcrumb mix until coated fully.
4. Add the breaded fillets to the preheated air-fryer and air-fry for 10 minutes. Check the internal temperature of the chicken has reached at least 74°C/165°F using a meat thermometer – if not, cook for another few minutes.
5. Serve with some additional sauce that has been warmed through.

Healthy Bang Bang Chicken

Servings: 4
Cooking Time:xx

Ingredients:

- 500g chicken breasts, cut into pieces of around 1" in size
- 1 beaten egg
- 50ml milk
- 1 tbsp hot pepper sauce
- 80g flour
- 70g tapioca starch
- 1 ½ tsp seasoned starch
- 1 tsp garlic granules
- ½ tsp cumin
- 6 tbsp plain Greek yogurt
- 3 tbsp sweet chilli sauce
- 1 tsp hot sauce

Directions:

1. Preheat the air fryer to 190°C
2. Take a mixing bowl and combine the egg, milk and

hot sauce
3. Take another bowl and combine the flour, tapioca starch, salt, garlic and cumin
4. Dip the chicken pieces into the sauce bowl and then into the flour bowl
5. Place the chicken into the air fryer
6. Whilst cooking, mix together the Greek yogurt, sweet chilli sauce and hot sauce and serve with the chicken

Bacon Wrapped Chicken Thighs

Servings: 4
Cooking Time:xx

Ingredients:

- 75g softened butter
- ½ clove minced garlic
- ¼ tsp dried thyme
- ¼ tsp dried basil
- ⅛ tsp coarse salt
- 100g thick cut bacon
- 350g chicken thighs, boneless and skinless
- 2 tsp minced garlic
- Salt and pepper to taste

Directions:

1. Take a mixing bowl and add the softened butter, garlic, thyme, basil, salt and pepper, combining well
2. Place the butter onto a sheet of plastic wrap and roll up to make a butter log
3. Refrigerate for about 2 hours
4. Remove the plastic wrap
5. Place one bacon strip onto the butter and then place the chicken thighs on top of the bacon. Sprinkle with garlic
6. Place the cold butter into the middle of the chicken thigh and tuck one end of bacon into the chicken
7. Next, fold over the chicken thigh whilst rolling the bacon around
8. Repeat with the rest
9. Preheat the air fryer to 188C
10. Cook the chicken until white in the centre and the juices run clear

Crispy Cornish Hen

Servings: 4
Cooking Time:xx

Ingredients:
- 2 Cornish hens, weighing around 500g each
- 2 tbsp olive oil
- 1 tsp garlic powder
- 1 tsp paprika
- 1.5 tsp Italian seasoning
- 1 tbsp lemon juice
- Salt and pepper to taste

Directions:
1. Preheat your air fryer to 260ºC
2. Combine all the ingredients into a bowl (except for the hens) until smooth
3. Brush the hens with the mixture, coating evenly
4. Place in the air fryer basket, with the breast side facing down
5. Cook for 35 minutes
6. Turn over and cook for another 10 minutes
7. Ensure the hens are white in the middle before serving

Buttermilk Chicken

Servings: 4
Cooking Time:xx

Ingredients:
- 500g chicken thighs, skinless and boneless
- 180ml buttermilk
- 40g tapioca flour
- ½ tsp garlic salt
- 1 egg
- 75g all purpose flour
- ½ tsp brown sugar
- 1 tsp garlic powder
- ½ tsp paprika
- ½ tsp onion powder
- ¼ tsp oregano
- Salt and pepper to taste

Directions:
1. Take a medium mixing bowl and combine the buttermilk and hot sauce
2. Add the tapioca flour, garlic salt and black pepper in a plastic bag and shake
3. Beat the egg
4. Take the chicken thighs and tip into the buttermilk, then the tapioca mixture, the egg, and then the flour

5. Preheat air fryer to 190ºC
6. Cook the chicken thighs for 10 minutes, until white in the middle

Chicken Balls, Greek-style

Servings: 4
Cooking Time:xx

Ingredients:
- 500g ground chicken
- 1 egg
- 1 tbsp dried oregano
- 1.5 tbsp garlic paste
- 1 tsp lemon zest
- 1 tsp dried onion powder
- Salt and pepper to taste

Directions:
1. Take a bowl and combine all ingredients well
2. Use your hands to create meatballs - you should be able to make 12 balls
3. Preheat your air fryer to 260ºC
4. Add the meatballs to the fryer and cook for 9 minutes

Chicken And Cheese Chimichangas

Servings: 6
Cooking Time:xx

Ingredients:
- 100g shredded chicken (cooked)
- 150g nacho cheese
- 1 chopped jalapeño pepper
- 6 flour tortillas
- 5 tbsp salsa
- 60g refried beans
- 1 tsp cumin
- 0.5 tsp chill powder
- Salt and pepper to taste

Directions:
1. Take a large mixing bowl and add all of the ingredients, combining well
2. Add ⅓ of the filling to each tortilla and roll into a burrito shape
3. Spray the air fryer with cooking spray and heat to 200ºC
4. Place the chimichangas in the air fryer and cook for 7 minutes

Pepper & Lemon Chicken Wings

Servings: 2
Cooking Time:xx

Ingredients:
- 1kg chicken wings
- 1/4 tsp cayenne pepper
- 2 tsp lemon pepper seasoning
- 3 tbsp butter
- 1 tsp honey
- An extra 1 tsp lemon pepper seasoning for the sauce

Directions:
1. Preheat the air fryer to 260ºC
2. Place the lemon pepper seasoning and cayenne in a bowl and combine
3. Coat the chicken in the seasoning
4. Place the chicken in the air fryer and cook for 20 minutes, turning over halfway
5. Turn the temperature up to 300ºC and cook for another 6 minutes
6. Meanwhile, melt the butter and combine with the honey and the rest of the seasoning
7. Remove the wings from the air fryer and pour the sauce over the top

Charred Chicken Breasts

Servings: 2
Cooking Time:xx

Ingredients:
- 2 tsp paprika
- 1 tsp ground thyme
- 1 tsp cumin
- ½ tsp cayenne pepper
- ½ tsp onion powder
- ½ tsp black pepper
- ¼ tsp salt
- 2 tsp vegetable oil
- 2 skinless boneless chicken breasts, cut into halves

Directions:
1. Take a bowl and add the paprika, thyme, cumin, cayenne pepper, onion powder, black pepper and salt
2. Coat each chicken breast with oil and dredge chicken in the spice mixture
3. Preheat air fryer to 175C
4. Cook for 10 minutes and flip
5. Cook for 10 more minutes

Air Fryer Chicken Thigh Schnitzel

Servings: 4
Cooking Time:xx

Ingredients:
- 300g boneless chicken thighs
- 160g seasoned breadcrumbs
- 1 tsp salt
- ½ tsp ground black pepper
- 30g flour
- 1 egg
- Cooking spray

Directions:
1. Lay the chicken on a sheet of parchment paper and add another on top
2. Use a mallet or a rolling pin to flatten it down
3. Take a bowl and add the breadcrumbs with the salt and pepper
4. Place the flour into another bowl
5. Dip the chicken into the flour, then the egg, and then the breadcrumbs
6. Preheat air fryer to 190ºC
7. Place the chicken into the air fryer and spray with cooking oil
8. Cook for 6 minutes

Turkey And Mushroom Burgers

Servings: 2
Cooking Time:xx

Ingredients:
- 180g mushrooms
- 500g minced turkey
- 1 tbsp of your favourite chicken seasoning, e.g. Maggi
- 1 tsp onion powder
- 1 tsp garlic powder
- Salt and pepper to taste

Directions:
1. Place the mushrooms in a food processor and puree
2. Add all the seasonings and mix well
3. Remove from the food processor and transfer to a mixing bowl
4. Add the minced turkey and combine again
5. Shape the mix into 5 burger patties
6. Spray with cooking spray and place in the air fryer
7. Cook at 160ºC for 10 minutes, until cooked.

Air Fryer Bbq Chicken

Servings: 4
Cooking Time:xx

Ingredients:

- 1 whole chicken
- 2 tbsp avocado oil
- 1 tbsp kosher salt
- 1 tsp ground pepper
- 1 tsp garlic powder
- 1 tsp paprika
- ½ tsp dried basil
- ½ tsp dried oregano
- ½ tsp dried thyme

Directions:

1. Mix the seasonings together and spread over chicken
2. Place the chicken in the air fryer breast side down
3. Cook at 182C for 50 minutes and then breast side up for 10 minutes
4. Carve and serve

Cornflake Chicken Nuggets

Servings: 4
Cooking Time:xx

Ingredients:

- 100 g/4 cups cornflakes (gluten-free if you wish)
- 70 g/½ cup plus ½ tablespoon plain/all-purpose flour (gluten-free if you wish)
- 2 eggs, beaten
- ½ teaspoon salt
- ¼ teaspoon freshly ground black pepper
- 600 g/1 lb. 5 oz. mini chicken fillets

Directions:

1. Grind the cornflakes in a food processor to a crumb-like texture. Place the flour in one bowl and the beaten eggs in a second bowl; season both bowls with the salt and pepper. Coat each chicken fillet in flour, tapping off any excess. Next dip each flour-coated chicken fillet into the egg, then the cornflakes until fully coated.
2. Preheat the air-fryer to 180°C/350°F.
3. Add the chicken fillets to the preheated air-fryer (you may need to add the fillets in two batches, depending on the size of your air-fryer) and air-fry for 10 minutes, turning halfway through cooking. Check the internal temperature of the nuggets has reached at least 74°C/165°F using a meat thermometer – if not, cook for another few minutes and then serve.

4. VARIATION: SIMPLE CHICKEN NUGGETS
5. For a simpler version, replace the crushed cornflakes with 90 g/1¼ cups dried breadcrumbs (see page 9). Prepare and air-fry in the same way.

Honey Cajun Chicken Thighs

Servings: 6
Cooking Time:xx

Ingredients:

- 100ml buttermilk
- 1 tsp hot sauce
- 400g skinless, boneless chicken thighs
- 150g all purpose flour
- 60g tapioca flour
- 2.5 tsp cajun seasoning
- ½ tsp garlic salt
- ½ tsp honey powder
- ¼ tsp ground paprika
- ⅛ tsp cayenne pepper
- 4 tsp honey

Directions:

1. Take a large bowl and combine the buttermilk and hot sauce
2. Transfer to a plastic bag and add the chicken thighs
3. Allow to marinate for 30 minutes
4. Take another bowl and add the flour, tapioca flour, cajun seasoning, garlic, salt, honey powder, paprika, and cayenne pepper, combining well
5. Dredge the chicken through the mixture
6. Preheat the air fryer to 175C
7. Cook for 15 minutes before flipping the thighs over and cooking for another 10 minutes
8. Drizzle 1 tsp of honey over each thigh

Buffalo Wings

Servings: 4
Cooking Time:xx

Ingredients:

- 500g chicken wings
- 1 tbsp olive oil
- 5 tbsp cayenne pepper sauce
- 75g butter
- 2 tbsp vinegar
- 1 tsp garlic powder
- ¼ tsp cayenne pepper

Directions:

1. Preheat the air fryer to 182C
2. Take a large mixing bowl and add the chicken

wings

3. Drizzle oil over the wings, coating evenly

4. Cook for 25 minutes and then flip the wings and cook for 5 more minutes

5. In a saucepan over a medium heat, mix the hot pepper sauce, butter, vinegar, garlic powder and cayenne pepper, combining well

6. Pour the sauce over the wings and flip to coat, before serving

Grain-free Chicken Katsu

Servings: 4
Cooking Time:xx

Ingredients:
- 125 g/1¼ cups ground almonds
- ½ teaspoon salt
- ½ teaspoon garlic powder
- ½ teaspoon dried parsley
- ½ teaspoon freshly ground black pepper
- ¼ teaspoon onion powder
- ¼ teaspoon dried oregano
- 450 g/1 lb. mini chicken fillets
- 1 egg, beaten
- oil, for spraying/drizzling
- coriander/cilantro leaves, to serve
- KATSU SAUCE
- 1 teaspoon olive oil or avocado oil
- 1 courgette/zucchini (approx. 150 g/5 oz.), finely chopped
- 1 carrot (approx. 100 g/3½ oz.), finely chopped
- 1 onion (approx. 120 g/4½ oz.), finely chopped
- 1 eating apple (approx. 150 g/5 oz.), cored and finely chopped
- 1 teaspoon ground ginger
- 1 teaspoon ground turmeric
- 2 teaspoons ground cumin
- 2 teaspoons ground coriander
- 1½ teaspoons mild chilli/chili powder
- 1 teaspoon garlic powder
- 1½ tablespoons runny honey
- 1 tablespoon soy sauce (gluten-free if you wish)
- 700 ml/3 cups vegetable stock (700 ml/3 cups water with 1½ stock cubes)

Directions:

1. First make the sauce. The easiest way to ensure all the vegetables and apple are finely chopped is to combine them in a food processor. Heat the oil in a large saucepan and sauté the finely chopped vegetables and apple for 5 minutes. Add all the seasonings, honey, soy sauce and stock and stir well, then bring to a simmer and simmer for 30 minutes.

2. Meanwhile, mix together the ground almonds, seasonings and spices. Dip each chicken fillet into the beaten egg, then into the almond-spice mix, making sure each fillet is fully coated. Spray the coated chicken fillets with olive oil (or simply drizzle over).

3. Preheat the air-fryer to 180ºC/350ºF.

4. Place the chicken fillets in the preheated air-fryer and air-fry for 10 minutes, turning halfway through cooking. Check the internal temperature of the chicken has reached at least 74ºC/165ºF using a meat thermometer – if not, cook for another few minutes.

5. Blend the cooked sauce in a food processor until smooth. Serve the chicken with the Katsu Sauce drizzled over (if necessary, reheat the sauce gently before serving) and scattered with coriander leaves. Any unused sauce can be frozen.

Chicken Tikka

Servings: 2
Cooking Time:xx

Ingredients:
- 2 chicken breasts, diced
- FIRST MARINADE
- freshly squeezed juice of ½ a lemon
- 1 tablespoon freshly grated ginger
- 1 tablespoon freshly grated garlic
- a good pinch of salt
- SECOND MARINADE
- 100 g/½ cup Greek yogurt
- ½ teaspoon chilli powder
- ½ teaspoon chilli paste
- ½ teaspoon turmeric
- ½ teaspoon garam masala
- 1 tablespoon olive oil

Directions:

1. Mix the ingredients for the first marinade together in a bowl, add in the chicken and stir to coat all the chicken pieces. Leave in the fridge to marinate for 20 minutes.

2. Combine the second marinade ingredients. Once the first marinade has had 20 minutes, add the second marinade to the chicken and stir well. Leave in the fridge for at least 4 hours.

3. Preheat the air-fryer to 180ºC/350ºF.

4. Thread the chicken pieces onto metal skewers that fit in your air-fryer. Add the skewers to the preheated air-fryer and air-fry for 10 minutes. Check the inter-

nal temperature of the chicken has reached at least 74°C/165°F using a meat thermometer – if not, cook for another few minutes and then serve.

Chicken Kiev

Servings: 4
Cooking Time:xx

Ingredients:
- 4 boneless chicken breasts
- 4 tablespoons plain/all-purpose flour (gluten-free if you wish)
- 1 egg, beaten
- 130 g/2 cups dried breadcrumbs (gluten-free if you wish, see page 9)
- GARLIC BUTTER
- 60 g/4 tablespoons salted butter, softened
- 1 large garlic clove, finely chopped

Directions:
1. Mash together the butter and garlic. Form into a sausage shape, then slice into 4 equal discs. Place in the freezer until frozen.
2. Make a deep horizontal slit across each chicken breast, taking care not to cut through to the other side. Stuff the cavity with a disc of frozen garlic butter. Place the flour in a shallow bowl, the egg in another and the breadcrumbs in a third. Coat each chicken breast first in flour, then egg, then breadcrumbs.
3. Preheat the air-fryer to 180°C/350°F.
4. Add the chicken Kievs to the preheated air-fryer and air-fry for 12 minutes until cooked through. This is hard to gauge as the butter inside the breast is not an indicator of doneness, so test the meat in the centre with a meat thermometer – it should be at least 75°C/167°F; if not, cook for another few minutes.

Chicken Jalfrezi

Servings: 4
Cooking Time:xx

Ingredients:
- 500g chicken breasts
- 1 tbsp water
- 4 tbsp tomato sauce
- 1 chopped onion
- 1 chopped bell pepper
- 2 tsp love oil
- 1 tsp turmeric
- 1 tsp cayenne pepper
- 2 tsp garam masala
- Salt and pepper to taste

Directions:
1. Take a large mixing bowl and add the chicken, onions, pepper, salt, garam masala, turmeric, oil and cayenne pepper, combining well
2. Place the chicken mix in the air fryer and cook at 180°C for 15 minutes
3. Take a microwave-safe bowl and add the tomato sauce, water salt, garam masala and cayenne, combining well
4. Cook in the microwave for 1 minute, stir then cook for a further minute
5. Remove the chicken from the air fryer and pour the sauce over the top.
6. Serve whilst still warm

Air Fryer Sesame Chicken Thighs

Servings: 4
Cooking Time:xx

Ingredients:
- 2 tbsp sesame oil
- 2 tbsp soy sauce
- 1 tbsp honey
- 1 tbsp sriracha sauce
- 1 tsp rice vinegar
- 400g chicken thighs
- 1 green onion, chopped
- 2 tbsp toasted sesame seeds

Directions:
1. Take a large bowl and combine the sesame oil, soy sauce, honey, sriracha and vinegar
2. Add the chicken and refrigerate for 30 minutes
3. Preheat the air fryer to 200°C
4. Cook for 5 minutes
5. Flip and then cook for another 10 minutes
6. Serve with green onion and sesame seeds

Buffalo Chicken Wontons

Servings: 6
Cooking Time:xx

Ingredients:
- 200g shredded chicken
- 1 tbsp buffalo sauce
- 4 tbsp softened cream cheese
- 1 sliced spring onion
- 2 tbsp blue cheese crumbles
- 12 wonton wrappers

Directions:

1. Preheat the air fryer to 200ºC
2. Take a bowl and combine the chicken and buffalo sauce
3. In another bowl mix the cream cheese until a smooth consistency has formed and then combine the scallion blue cheese and seasoned chicken
4. Take the wonton wrappers and run wet fingers along each edge
5. Place 1 tbsp of the filling into the centre of the wonton and fold the corners together
6. Cook at 200ºC for 3 to 5 minutes, until golden brown

Chicken Fried Rice

Servings: 4
Cooking Time:xx

Ingredients:

- 400g cooked white rice
- 400g cooked chicken, diced
- 200g frozen peas and carrots
- 6 tbsp soy sauce
- 1 tbsp vegetable oil
- 1 diced onion

Directions:

1. Take a large bowl and add the rice, vegetable oil and soy sauce and combine well
2. Add the frozen peas, carrots, diced onion and the chicken and mix together well
3. Pour the mixture into a nonstick pan
4. Place the pan into the air fryer
5. Cook at 182C for 20 minutes

Bbq Chicken Tenders

Servings: 6
Cooking Time:xx

Ingredients:

- 300g barbecue flavoured pork rinds
- 200g all purpose flour
- 1 tbsp barbecue seasoning
- 1 egg
- 400g chicken breast tenderloins
- Cooking spray

Directions:

1. Preheat the air fryer to 190ºC
2. Place the pork rinds into a food processor and blitz to a breadcrumb consistency, before transferring to a bowl

3. In a separate bowl, combine the flour and barbecue seasoning
4. Beat the egg in a small bowl
5. Take the chicken and first dip into the egg, then the flour, and then the breadcrumbs
6. Place the chicken into the air fryer and spray with cooking spray and cook for about 15 minutes

Chicken Milanese

Servings: 4
Cooking Time:xx

Ingredients:

- 130 g/1¾ cups dried breadcrumbs (gluten-free if you wish, see page 9)
- 50 g/⅔ cup grated Parmesan
- 1 teaspoon dried basil
- ½ teaspoon dried thyme
- ¼ teaspoon freshly ground black pepper
- 1 egg, beaten
- 4 tablespoons plain/all-purpose flour (gluten-free if you wish)
- 4 boneless chicken breasts

Directions:

1. Combine the breadcrumbs, cheese, herbs and pepper in a bowl. In a second bowl beat the egg, and in the third bowl have the plain/all-purpose flour. Dip each chicken breast first into the flour, then the egg, then the seasoned breadcrumbs.
2. Preheat the air-fryer to 180ºC/350ºF.
3. Add the breaded chicken breasts to the preheated air-fryer and air-fry for 12 minutes. Check the internal temperature of the chicken has reached at least 74ºC/165ºF using a meat thermometer – if not, cook for another few minutes.

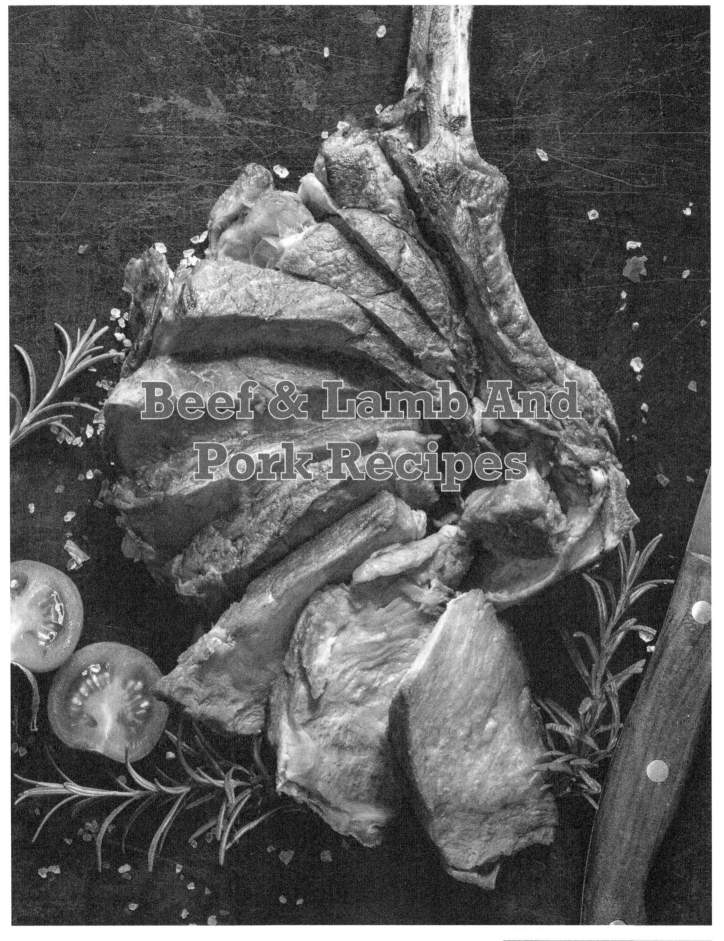

Beef & Lamb And Pork Recipes

Beef & Lamb And Pork Recipes

Hamburgers

Servings: 4
Cooking Time:xx

Ingredients:
- 500g minced beef
- 1 grated onion
- Salt and pepper to taste

Directions:
1. Preheat air fryer to 200ºC
2. Place the grated onion and the beef into a bowl and combine together well
3. Divide minced beef into 4 equal portions, form into patties
4. Season with salt and pepper
5. Place in the air fryer and cook for 10 minutes, turnover and cook for a further 3 minutes

Traditional Empanadas

Servings: 2
Cooking Time:xx

Ingredients:
- 300g minced beef
- 1 tbsp olive oil
- ¼ cup finely chopped onion
- 150g chopped mushrooms
- ⅛ tsp cinnamon
- 4 chopped tomatoes
- 2 tsp chopped garlic
- 6 green olives
- ¼ tsp paprika
- ¼ tsp cumin
- 8 goyoza wrappers
- 1 beaten egg

Directions:
1. Heat oil in a pan add onion and minced beef and cook until browned
2. Add mushrooms and cook for 6 minutes
3. Add garlic, olives, paprika, cumin and cinnamon, and cook for about 3 minutes
4. Stir in tomatoes and cook for 1 minute, set aside allow to cool
5. Place 1 ½ tbsp of filling in each goyoza wrapper

6. Brush edges with egg fold over and seal pinching edges
7. Place in the air fryer and cook at 200 for about 7 minutes

Breaded Pork Chops

Servings: 6
Cooking Time:xx

Ingredients:
- 6 boneless pork chops
- 1 beaten egg
- 100g panko crumbs
- 75g crushed cornflakes
- 2 tbsp parmesan
- 1 ¼ tsp paprika
- ½ tsp garlic powder
- ½ tsp onion powder
- ¼ tsp chilli powder
- Salt and pepper to taste

Directions:
1. Heat the air fryer to 200ºC
2. Season the pork chops with salt
3. Mix the panko, cornflakes, salt, parmesan, garlic powder, onion powder, paprika, chilli powder and pepper in a bowl
4. Beat the egg in another bowl
5. Dip the pork in the egg and then coat with panko mix
6. Place in the air fryer and cook for about 12 minutes turning halfway

Asparagus & Steak Parcels

Servings: 4
Cooking Time:xx

Ingredients:
- 500g flank steak, cut into 6 equal pieces
- 75ml Tamari sauce
- 2 crushed garlic cloves
- 250g trimmed asparagus
- 3 large bell peppers, thinly sliced
- 2 tbsp butter
- Salt and pepper to taste

Directions:
1. Season the steak to your liking
2. Place the meat in a zip top bag and add the Tamari and garlic, sealing the bag closed
3. Make sure the steaks are fully coated in the sauce and leave them in the fright at least 1 hour, but preferably overnight
4. Remove the steaks from the bag and throw the marinade away
5. Place the peppers and sliced asparagus in the centre of each steak piece
6. Roll the steak up and secure in place with a tooth pick
7. Preheat your air fryer to 250ºC
8. Transfer the meat parcels to the air fryer and cook for 5 minutes
9. Allow to rest before serving
10. Melt the butter in a saucepan, over a medium heat, adding the juices from the air fryer
11. Combine well and keep cooking until thickened
12. Pour the sauce over the steak parcels and season to your liking

Italian Meatballs

Servings: 12
Cooking Time:xx

Ingredients:
- 2 tbsp olive oil
- 2 tbsp minced shallot
- 3 cloves garlic minced
- 100g panko crumbs
- 35g chopped parsley
- 1 tbsp chopped rosemary
- 60ml milk
- 400g minced pork
- 250g turkey sausage
- 1 egg beaten
- 1 tbsp dijon mustard
- 1 tbsp finely chopped thyme

Directions:
1. Preheat air fryer to 200ºC
2. Heat oil in a pan and cook the garlic and shallot over a medium heat for 1-2 minutes
3. Mix the panko and milk in a bowl and allow to stand for 5 minutes
4. Add all the ingredients to the panko mix and combine well
5. Shape into 1 ½ inch meatballs and cook for 12 minutes

Cheesy Meatballs

Servings: 2
Cooking Time:xx

Ingredients:
- 500g ground beef
- 1 can of chopped green chillis
- 1 egg white
- 1 tbsp water
- 2 tbsp taco seasoning
- 16 pieces of pepper jack cheese, cut into cubes
- 300g nacho cheese tortilla chips, crushed
- 6 tbsp taco sauce
- 3 tbsp honey

Directions:
1. Take a large bowl and combine the beef with the green collie sand taco seasoning
2. Use your hands to create meatballs - you should get around 15 balls in total
3. Place a cube of cheese in the middle of each meatball, forming the ball around it once more
4. Take a small bowl and beat the egg white
5. Take a large bowl and add the crushed chips
6. Dip every meatball into the egg white and then the crushed chips
7. Place the balls into the air fryer and cook at 260ºC for 14 minutes, turning halfway
8. Take a microwave-safe bowl and combine the honey and taco sauce
9. Place in the microwave for 30 seconds and serve the sauce warm with the meatballs

Japanese Pork Chops

Servings: 4
Cooking Time:xx

Ingredients:
- 6 boneless pork chops
- 30g flour
- 2 beaten eggs
- 2 tbsp sweet chilli sauce
- 500g cup seasoned breadcrumbs
- ⅛ tsp salt
- ⅛ tsp pepper
- Tonkatsu sauce to taste

Directions:
1. Place the flour, breadcrumbs and eggs in 3 separate bowls
2. Sprinkle both sides of the pork with salt and pepper

3. Coat the pork in flour, egg and then breadcrumbs

4. Place in the air fryer and cook at 180ºC for 8 minutes, turn then cook for a further 5 minutes

5. Serve with sauces on the side

Tahini Beef Bites

Servings: 2
Cooking Time:xx

Ingredients:
- 500g sirloin steak, cut into cubes
- 2 tbsp Za'atar seasoning
- 1 tsp olive oil
- 25g Tahini
- 25g warm water
- 1 tbsp lemon juice
- 1 clove of garlic
- Salt to taste

Directions:
1. Preheat the air fryer to 250ºC

2. Take a bowl and combine the oil with the steak, salt, and Za'atar seasoning

3. Place in the air fryer and cook for 10 minutes, turning halfway through

4. Take a bowl and combine the water, garlic, lemon juice, salt, and tahini, or use a food processor if you have one

5. Pour the sauce over the bites and serve

Jamaican Jerk Pork

Servings: 4
Cooking Time:xx

Ingredients:
- 400g pork butt cut into 3 pieces
- 100g jerk paste

Directions:
1. Rub the pork with jerk paste and marinate for 4 hours

2. Preheat air fryer to 190ºC

3. Place pork in the air fryer and cook for about 20 minutes turning halfway

Sweet And Sticky Ribs

Servings:2
Cooking Time:1 Hour 15 Minutes

Ingredients:
- 500 g / 17.6 oz pork ribs
- 2 cloves garlic, minced

- 2 tbsp soy sauce
- 2 tsp honey
- 1 tbsp cayenne pepper
- 1 tsp olive oil
- 2 tbsp BBQ sauce
- 1 tsp salt
- 1 tsp black pepper

Directions:
1. Place the pork ribs on a clean surface and cut them into smaller chunks if necessary.

2. In a small mixing bowl, combine the minced garlic, soy sauce, 1 tsp honey, cayenne pepper, olive oil, BBQ sauce, salt, and pepper. Rub the pork ribs into the sauce and spice the mixture until fully coated.

3. Place the coated ribs in the fridge for 1 hour. Meanwhile, preheat the air fryer to 180 °C / 350 °F and line the bottom of the basket with parchment paper.

4. After one hour, transfer the pork ribs into the prepared air fryer basket. Close the lid and cook for 15 minutes, using tongs to turn them halfway through.

5. Once cooked, remove the ribs from the air fryer and use a brush to top each rib with the remaining 1 tsp honey.

6. Return the ribs to the air fryer for a further 2-3 minutes to heat the honey glaze before serving.

Cheese & Ham Sliders

Servings: 4
Cooking Time:xx

Ingredients:
- 8 slider bread rolls, cut in half
- 16 slices of sweet ham
- 16 slices of Swiss cheese
- 5 tbsp mayonnaise
- 1/2 tsp paprika
- 1 tsp onion powder
- 1 tsp dill

Directions:
1. Place 2 slices of ham into each bread roll and 2 slices of cheese

2. Take a bowl and combine the mayonnaise with the onion powder, dill and paprika

3. Add half a tablespoon of the sauce on top of each piece of cheese

4. Place the top on the bread slider

5. Cook at 220ºC for 5 minutes

Mustard Glazed Pork

Servings: 4
Cooking Time:xx

Ingredients:
- 500g pork tenderloin
- 1 tbsp minced garlic
- ¼ tsp salt
- ⅛ tsp cracked black pepper
- 75g yellow mustard
- 3 tbsp brown sugar
- 1 tsp Italian seasoning
- 1 tsp rosemary

Directions:
1. Cut slits into the pork place the minced garlic into the slits, season with the salt and pepper
2. Add the remaining ingredients to a bowl and whisk to combine
3. Rub the mix over the pork and allow to marinate for 2 hours
4. Place in the air fryer and cook at 200ºC for 20 minutes

Pork Taquitos

Servings: 5
Cooking Time:xx

Ingredients:
- 400g shredded pork
- 500g grated mozzarella
- 10 flour tortillas
- The juice of 1 lime
- Cooking spray

Directions:
1. Preheat air fryer to 190ºC
2. Sprinkle lime juice on the pork and mix
3. Microwave tortilla for about 10 seconds to soften
4. Add a little pork and cheese to a tortilla
5. Roll then tortilla up, and place in the air fryer
6. Cook for about 7 minutes until golden, turn halfway through cooking

Char Siu Buffalo

Servings: 2
Cooking Time:xx

Ingredients:
- 1 kg beef, cut into strips
- 4 tbsp honey
- 2 tbsp sugar
- 2 tbsp char siu sauce
- 2 tbsp oyster sauce
- 2 tbsp soy sauce
- 2 tbsp olive oil
- 2 tsp minced garlic
- ¼ tsp bi carbonate of soda

Directions:
1. Place all the ingredients in a bowl, mix well and marinate over night
2. Line the air fryer with foil, add the beef, keep the marinade to one side
3. Cook at 200ºC for 10 minutes
4. Brush the pork with the sauce and cook for another 20 minutes at 160ºC
5. Remove the meat and set aside
6. Strain the marinade into a saucepan, heat until it thickens
7. Drizzle over the pork and serve with rice

Pork Chilli Cheese Dogs

Servings: 2
Cooking Time:xx

Ingredients:
- 1 can of pork chilli, or chilli you have left over
- 200g grated cheese
- 2 hot dog bread rolls
- 2 hot dogs

Directions:
1. Preheat the air fryer to 260ºC
2. Cook the hot dogs for 4 minutes, turning halfway
3. Place the hotdogs inside the bread rolls and place back inside the air fryer
4. Top with half the cheese on top and then the chilli
5. Add the rest of the cheese
6. Cook for an extra 2 minutes

Hamburgers With Feta

Servings: 4
Cooking Time.xx

Ingredients:
- 400g minced beef
- 250g crumbled feta
- 25g chopped green olives
- ½ tsp garlic powder
- ½ cup chopped onion
- 2 tbsp Worcestershire sauce
- ½ tsp steak seasoning
- Salt to taste

Directions:
1. Mix all the ingredients in a bowl
2. Divide the mix into four and shape into patties
3. Place in the air fryer and cook at 200°C for about 15 minutes

Pizza Dogs

Servings: 2
Cooking Time:xx

Ingredients:
- 2 pork hot dogs
- 4 pepperoni slices, halved
- 150g pizza sauce
- 2 hotdog buns
- 75g grated cheese
- 2 tsp sliced olives

Directions:
1. Preheat air fryer to 190°C
2. Place 4 slits down each hotdog, place in the air fryer and cook for 3 minutes
3. Place a piece of pepperoni into each slit, add pizza sauce to hot dog buns
4. Place hotdogs in the buns and top with cheese and olives
5. Cook in the air fryer for about 2 minutes

Chinese Pork With Pineapple

Servings: 4
Cooking Time:xx

Ingredients:
- 450g pork loin, cubed
- ½ tsp salt
- ½ tsp pepper
- 1 tbsp brown sugar
- 75g fresh coriander, chopped
- 2 tbsp toasted sesame seeds
- ½ pineapple, cubed
- 1 sliced red pepper
- 1 minced clove of garlic
- 1 tsp ginger
- 2 tbsp soy
- 1 tbsp oil

Directions:
1. Season the pork with salt and pepper
2. Add all ingredients to the air fryer
3. Cook at 180°C for 17 minutes
4. Serve and garnish with coriander and toasted sesame seeds

Buttermilk Pork Chops

Servings: 4
Cooking Time:xx

Ingredients:
- 4 pork chops
- 3 tbsp buttermilk
- 75g flour
- Cooking oil spray
- 1 packet of pork rub
- Salt and pepper to taste

Directions:
1. Rub the chops with the pork rub
2. Place the pork chops in a bowl and drizzle with buttermilk
3. Coat the chops with flour
4. Place in the air fryer and cook at 190°C for 15 minutes turning halfway

Steak Dinner

Servings: 5
Cooking Time:xx

Ingredients:
- 400g sirloin steak, cut into cubes
- 300g red potatoes, cubed
- 1 pepper
- 1 tsp dried parsley
- ½ tsp pepper
- 2 tsp olive oil
- 1 sliced onion
- 300g chopped mushrooms
- 2 tsp garlic salt
- 2 tsp salt
- 5 tsp butter

Directions:
1. Preheat the air fryer to 200°C
2. Take 5 pieces of foil, layer meat onion, potatoes, mushrooms and pepper in each one
3. Add 1 tsp of butter to each one
4. Mix seasonings and sprinkle over the top
5. Fold the foil and cook for 25-30 minutes

Roast Beef

Servings: 2
Cooking Time:xx

Ingredients:
- 400g beef fillet
- 1 tbsp olive oil
- 1 tsp salt
- 1 tsp rosemary

Directions:
1. Preheat the air fryer to 180°C
2. Mix salt, rosemary and oil on a plate
3. Coat the beef with the mix
4. Place the beef in the air fryer and cook for 45 minutes turning halfway

Carne Asada Chips

Servings: 2
Cooking Time:xx

Ingredients:
- 500g sirloin steak
- 1 bag of frozen French fries
- 350g grated cheese
- 2 tbsp sour cream
- 2 tbsp guacamole
- 2 tbsp steak seasoning
- Salt and pepper to taste

Directions:
1. Preheat your oven to 260°C
2. Season the steak with the seasoning and a little salt and pepper
3. Place in the air fryer and cook for 4 minutes, before turning over and cooking for another 4 minutes
4. Remove and allow to rest
5. Add the French fries to the fryer and cook for 5 minutes, shaking regularly
6. Add the cheese
7. Cut the steak into pieces and add on top of the cheese
8. Cook for another 30 seconds, until the cheese is melted
9. Season

Copycat Burger

Servings: 4
Cooking Time:xx

Ingredients:
- 400g minced pork
- 4 wholemeal burger buns
- Avocado sauce to taste
- 1 avocado
- 1 small onion, chopped
- 2 chopped spring onions
- Salad garnish
- 1 tbsp Worcester sauce
- 1 tbsp tomato ketchup
- 1 tsp garlic puree
- 1 tsp mixed herbs

Directions:
1. In a bowl mix together the mince, onion, half the avocado and all of the seasoning
2. Form into burgers
3. Place in the air fryer and cook at 180°C for 8 minutes
4. When cooked place in the bun, layer with sauce and salad garnish

Pork Schnitzel

Servings: 2
Cooking Time:xx

Ingredients:
- 3 pork steaks, cut into cubes
- Salt and pepper
- 175g flour
- 2 eggs
- 175g breadcrumbs

Directions:
1. Sprinkle the pork with salt and pepper
2. Coat in the flour then dip in the egg
3. Coat the pork in breadcrumbs
4. Place in the air fryer and cook at 175°C for 20 minutes turning halfway
5. Serve with red cabbage

Beef Kebobs

Servings: 4
Cooking Time:xx

Ingredients:
- 500g cubed beef
- 25g low fat sour cream
- 2 tbsp soy sauce
- 8 x 6 inch skewers
- 1 bell pepper
- Half an onion

Directions:
1. Mix the sour cream and soy sauce in a bowl, add the cubed beef and marinate for at least 30 minutes
2. Cut the pepper and onion into 1 inch pieces, soak the skewers in water for 10 minutes
3. Thread beef, bell peppers and onion onto skewers
4. Cook in the air fryer at 200ºC for 10 minutes turning halfway

Roast Pork

Servings: 4
Cooking Time:xx

Ingredients:
- 500g pork joint
- 1 tbsp olive oil
- 1 tsp salt

Directions:
1. Preheat air fryer to 180ºC
2. Score the pork skin with a knife
3. Drizzle the pork with oil and rub it into the skin, sprinkle with salt
4. Place in the air fryer and cook for about 50 minutes

Steak Fajitas

Servings: 4
Cooking Time:xx

Ingredients:
- 500g sliced steak
- 25g pineapple juice
- 2 tbsp lime juice
- 1 tbsp olive oil
- 1 tbsp soy sauce
- 1 tbsp minced garlic
- ½ tbsp chilli powder
- 1/2 tsp paprika
- 1 tsp cumin
- 1 pepper
- 1 onion
- Salt and pepper to taste

Directions:
1. Mix pineapple juice, lime juice, olive oil, soy sauce, garlic, cumin chilli powder and paprika. Pour over the steak and marinate for 4 hours
2. Line the air fryer with foil, add the peppers and onions, season with salt and pepper
3. Cook at 200ºC for 10 minutes, add the steak and cook for another 7 minutes
4. Serve with tortillas
5. Set your fryer to 170ºC and cook the sandwich for 4 minutes
6. Turn the sandwich over and cook for another 3 minutes
7. Turn the sandwich out and serve whilst hot
8. Repeat with the other remaining sandwich

Pork Chops With Raspberry And Balsamic

Servings: 4
Cooking Time:xx

Ingredients:
- 2 large eggs
- 30ml milk
- 250g panko bread crumbs
- 250g finely chopped pecans
- 1 tbsp orange juice
- 4 pork chops
- 30ml balsamic vinegar
- 2 tbsp brown sugar
- 2 tbsp raspberry jam

Directions:
1. Preheat air fryer to 200ºC
2. Mix the eggs and milk together in a bowl
3. In another bowl mix the breadcrumbs and pecans
4. Coat the pork chops in flour, egg and then coat in the breadcrumbs
5. Place in the air fryer and cook for 12 minutes until golden turning halfway
6. Put the remaining ingredients in a pan simmer for about 6 minutes, serve with the pork chops

Beef Nacho Pinwheels

Servings: 6
Cooking Time:xx

Ingredients:
- 500g minced beef
- 1 packet of taco seasoning
- 300ml water
- 300ml sour cream
- 6 tostadas
- 6 flour tortillas
- 3 tomatoes
- 250g nacho cheese
- 250g shredded lettuce
- 250g Mexican cheese

Directions:
1. Preheat air fryer to 200ºC
2. Brown the mince in a pan and add the taco seasoning
3. Share the remaining ingredients between the tortillas
4. Fold the edges of the tortillas up towards the centre, should look like a pinwheel
5. Lay seam down in the air fryer and cook for 2 minutes
6. Turnover and cook for a further 2 minutes

Homemade Crispy Pepperoni Pizza

Servings:4
Cooking Time:10 Minutes

Ingredients:
- For the pizza dough:
- 500 g / 17.6 oz plain flour
- 1 tsp salt
- 1 tsp dry non-fast-acting yeast
- 400 ml warm water
- For the toppings:
- 100 g / 3.5 oz tomato sauce
- 100 g / 3.5 oz mozzarella cheese, grated
- 8 slices pepperoni

Directions:
1. To make the pizza dough, place the plain flour, salt, and dry yeast in a large mixing bowl. Pour in the warm water bit by bit until it forms a tacky dough.
2. Lightly dust a clean kitchen top surface with plain flour and roll the dough out until it is around ½ an inch thick.
3. Preheat your air fryer to 150 °C / 300 °F and line the bottom of the basket with parchment paper.
4. Spread the tomato sauce evenly across the dough and top with grated mozzarella cheese. Top with the pepperoni slices and carefully transfer the pizza into the lined air fryer basket.
5. Cook the pizza until the crust is golden and crispy, and the mozzarella cheese has melted.
6. Enjoy the pizza while still hot with a side salad and some potato wedges.

Steak Popcorn Bites

Servings: 4
Cooking Time:xx

Ingredients:
- 500g steak, cut into 1" sized cubes
- 500g potato chips, ridged ones work best
- 100g flour
- 2 beaten eggs
- Salt and pepper to taste

Directions:
1. Place the chips into the food processor and pulse unit you get fine chip crumbs
2. Take a bowl and combine the flour with salt and pepper
3. Add the chips to another bowl and the beaten egg to another bowl
4. Take the steak cubes and dip first in the flour, then the egg and then the chip crumbs
5. Preheat your air fryer to 260ºC
6. Place the steak pieces into the fryer and cook for 9 minutes

Fish & Seafood Recipes

Fish & Seafood Recipes

Chilli Lime Tilapia

Servings: 3
Cooking Time:xx

Ingredients:
- 500g Tilapia fillets
- 25g panko crumbs
- 200g flour
- Salt and pepper to taste
- 2 eggs
- 1 tbsp chilli powder
- The juice of 1 lime

Directions:
1. Mix panko, salt and pepper and chilli powder together
2. Whisk the egg in a separate bowl
3. Spray the air fryer with cooking spray
4. Dip the tilapia in the flour, then in the egg and cover in the panko mix
5. Place fish in the air fryer, spray with cooking spray and cook for 7-8 minutes at 190ºC
6. Turn the fish over and cook for a further 7-8 minutes until golden brown.
7. Squeeze lime juice over the top and serve

Mushrooms Stuffed With Crab

Servings: 2
Cooking Time:xx

Ingredients:
- 500g large mushrooms
- 2 tsp salt
- Half a diced red onion
- 2 diced celery sticks
- 300g lump crab
- 35g seasoned breadcrumbs
- 1 egg
- 1 tsp oregano
- 1 tsp hot sauce
- 50g grated Parmesan cheese

Directions:
1. Preheat to 260ºC
2. Take a baking sheet and arrange the mushrooms top down

3. Spray with a little cooking oil
4. Take a bowl and combine the onions, celery, breadcrumbs, egg, crab and half the cheese, oregano and hot sauce
5. Fill each mushroom with the mixture and make sure it's heaped over the top
6. Cover with the rest of the cheese
7. Place in the air fryer for 18 minutes

Thai Fish Cakes

Servings: 4
Cooking Time:xx

Ingredients:
- 200g pre-mashed potatoes
- 2 fillets of white fish, flaked and mashed
- 1 onion
- 1 tsp butter
- 1 tsp milk
- 1 lime zest and rind
- 3 tsp chilli
- 1 tsp Worcester sauce
- 1 tsp coriander
- 1 tsp mixed spice
- 1 tsp mixed herbs
- 50g breadcrumbs
- Salt and pepper to taste

Directions:
1. Cover the white fish in milk
2. in a mixing bowl place the fish and add the seasoning and mashed potatoes
3. Add the butter and remaining milk
4. Use your hands to create patties and place in the refrigerator for 3 hours
5. Preheat your air fryer to 200ºC
6. Cook for 15 minutes

Cod Nuggets

Servings: 4
Cooking Time:xx

Ingredients:
- 400g cod fillets, cut into 8 chunks
- 35g flour
- 1 tbsp vegetable oil
- 200g cornflakes or cracker crumbs
- Egg wash - 1 tbsp egg and 1 tbsp water
- Salt and pepper to taste

Directions:
1. Crush the crackers or cornflakes to make crumbs, mix in the vegetable oil
2. Season the cod with salt and pepper and cover in flour, dip into the egg-wash then cover in crumbs
3. Set the air fryer to 180ºC
4. Place the cod nuggets in the air fryer basket and cook for 15 minutes, until golden brown.

Lobster Tails

Servings: 2
Cooking Time:xx

Ingredients:
- 4 lobster tails
- 2 tbsp melted butter
- ½ tsp salt
- 1 tsp pepper

Directions:
1. Cut the lobster tails through the tail section and pull back the shell
2. Brush with the melted butter and sprinkle with salt and pepper
3. Heat the air fryer to 200ºC and cook for 4 minutes
4. Brush with melted butter and cook for a further 2 minutes

Ranch Style Fish Fillets

Servings: 4
Cooking Time:xx

Ingredients:
- 200g bread crumbs
- 30g ranch-style dressing mix
- 2 tbsp oil
- 2 beaten eggs
- 4 fish fillets of your choice
- Lemon wedges to garnish

Directions:
1. Preheat air fryer to 180ºC
2. Mix the bread crumbs and ranch dressing mix together, add in the oil until the mix becomes crumbly
3. Dip the fish into the, then cover in the breadcrumb mix
4. Place in the air fryer and cook for 12-13 minutes

Maine Seafood

Servings: 2
Cooking Time:xx

Ingredients:
- 500g flour
- 400g breadcrumbs
- 300g steamer clams
- 3 eggs
- 3 tbsp water

Directions:
1. Soak the clams for 3 hours, drain and rinse
2. Bring 1 inch of water to boil, add the clams and cover with a lid, steam for about 7 minutes until the clams open.
3. Remove the clams from the shell and set aside
4. Put the eggs in a bowl and mix with the water
5. Dip the clams in the flour, then the egg and then coat in breadcrumbs
6. Heat the air fryer to 180ºC and cook for about 7 minutes

Oat & Parmesan Crusted Fish Fillets

Servings: 2
Cooking Time:xx

Ingredients:
- 20 g/⅓ cup fresh breadcrumbs
- 25 g/3 tablespoons oats
- 15 g/¼ cup grated Parmesan
- 1 egg
- 2 x 175-g/6-oz. white fish fillets, skin-on
- salt and freshly ground black pepper

Directions:
1. Preheat the air-fryer to 180°C/350°F.
2. Combine the breadcrumbs, oats and cheese in a bowl and stir in a pinch of salt and pepper. In another bowl beat the egg. Dip the fish fillets in the egg, then top with the oat mixture.
3. Add the fish fillets to the preheated air-fryer on an air-fryer liner or a piece of pierced parchment paper. Air-fry for 10 minutes. Check the fish is just flaking away when a fork is inserted, then serve immediately.

Fish Sticks With Tartar Sauce Batter

Servings: 4
Cooking Time:xx

Ingredients:
- 6 tbsp mayonnaise
- 2 tbsp dill pickle
- 1 tsp seafood seasoning
- 400g cod fillets, cut into sticks
- 300g panko breadcrumbs

Directions:
1. Combine the mayonnaise, seafood seasoning and dill pickle in a large bowl.
2. Add the cod sticks and coat well
3. Preheat air fryer to 200°C
4. Coat the fish sticks in the breadcrumbs
5. Place in the air fryer and cook for 12 minutes

Cajun Shrimp Boil

Servings: 6
Cooking Time:xx

Ingredients:
- 300g cooked shrimp
- 14 slices of smoked sausage
- 5 par boiled potatoes, cut into halves
- 4 mini corn on the cobs, quartered
- 1 diced onion
- 3 tbsp old bay seasoning
- Olive oil spray

Directions:
1. Combine all the ingredients in a bowl and mix well
2. Line the air fryer with foil
3. Place half the mix into the air fryer and cook at 200°C for about 6 minutes, mix the ingredients and cook for a further 6 minutes.
4. Repeat for the second batch

Lemon Pepper Shrimp

Servings: 2
Cooking Time:xx

Ingredients:
- ½ tbsp olive oil
- The juice of 1 lemon
- ¼ tsp paprika
- 1 tsp lemon pepper
- ¼ tsp garlic powder
- 400g uncooked shrimp
- 1 sliced lemon

Directions:
1. Preheat air fryer to 200°C
2. Mix olive oil, lemon juice, paprika, lemon pepper and garlic powder. Add the shrimp and mix well
3. Place shrimp in the air fryer and cook for 6-8 minutes until pink and firm.
4. Serve with lemon slices

Traditional Fish And Chips

Servings: 4
Cooking Time:xx

Ingredients:
- 4 potatoes, peeled and cut into chips
- 2 fish fillets of your choice
- 1 beaten egg
- 3 slices of wholemeal bread, grated into breadcrumbs
- 25g tortilla crisps
- 1 lemon rind and juice
- 1 tbsp parsley
- Salt and pepper to taste

Directions:
1. Preheat your air fryer to 200°C
2. Place the chips inside and cook until crispy
3. Cut the fish fillets into 4 slices and season with lemon juice
4. Place the breadcrumbs, lemon rind, parsley, tortillas and seasoning into a food processor and blitz to create a crumb consistency
5. Place the breadcrumbs on a large plate
6. Coat the fish in the egg and then the breadcrumb mixture
7. Cook for 15 minutes at 180°C

Baked Panko Cod

Servings: 5
Cooking Time:xx

Ingredients:
- 400g cod, cut into 5 pieces
- 250g panko breadcrumbs
- 1 egg plus 1 egg white extra
- Cooking spray
- ½ tsp onion powder
- ½ tsp garlic salt
- ⅛ tsp black pepper
- ½ tsp mixed herbs

Directions:
1. Heat air fryer to 220°C
2. Beat the egg and egg white in a bowl
3. Sprinkle fish with herbs and spice mix, dip into the egg and then cover in the panko bread crumbs
4. Line air fryer basket with tin foil. Place the fish in the air fryer and coat with cooking spray
5. Cook for about 15 minutes until, fish is lightly browned

Coconut Shrimp

Servings: 4
Cooking Time:xx

Ingredients:
- 250g flour
- 1 ½ tsp black pepper
- 2 eggs
- 150g unsweetened flaked coconut
- 1 Serrano chilli, thinly sliced
- 25g panko bread crumbs
- 300g shrimp raw
- ½ tsp salt
- 4 tbsp honey
- 25ml lime juice

Directions:
1. Mix together flour and pepper, in another bowl beat the eggs and in another bowl mix the panko and coconut
2. Dip each of the shrimp in the flour mix then the egg and then cover in the coconut mix
3. Coat the shrimp in cooking spray
4. Place in the air fryer and cook at 200°C for 6-8 mins turning half way through
5. Mix together the honey, lime juice and chilli and serve with the shrimp

Garlic Tilapia

Servings: 2
Cooking Time:xx

Ingredients:
- 2 tilapia fillets
- 2 tsp chopped fresh chives
- 2 tsp chopped fresh parsley
- 2 tsp olive oil
- 1 tsp minced garlic
- Salt and pepper for seasoning

Directions:
1. Preheat the air fryer to 220°C
2. Take a small bowl and combine the olive oil with the chives, garlic, parsley and a little salt and pepper
3. Brush the mixture over the fish fillets
4. Place the fish into the air fryer and cook for 10 minutes, until flaky

Tilapia Fillets

Servings: 2
Cooking Time:xx

Ingredients:
- 2 tbsp melted butter
- 150g almond flour
- 3 tbsp mayonnaise
- 2 tilapia fillets
- 25g thinly sliced almonds
- Salt and pepper to taste
- Vegetable oil spray

Directions:
1. Mix the almond flour, butter, pepper and salt together in a bowl
2. Spread mayonnaise on both sides of the fish
3. Cover the fillets in the almond flour mix
4. Spread one side of the fish with the sliced almonds
5. Spray the air fryer with the vegetable spray
6. Place in the air fryer and cook at 160°C for 10 minutes

Shrimp Wrapped With Bacon

Servings: 2
Cooking Time:xx

Ingredients:
- 16 shrimp
- 16 slices of bacon
- 2 tbsp ranch dressing to serve

Directions:
1. Preheat the air fryer to 200°C
2. Wrap the shrimps in the bacon
3. Refrigerate for 30 minutes
4. Cook the shrimp for about 5 minutes turn them over and cook for a further 2 minutes
5. Serve with the ranch dressing on the side

Crispy Nacho Prawns

Servings: 6
Cooking Time:xx

Ingredients:
- 1 egg
- 18 large prawns
- 1 bag of nacho cheese flavoured corn chips, crushed

Directions:
1. Wash the prawns and pat dry
2. Place the chips into a bowl
3. In another bowl, whisk the egg
4. Dip the prawns into the egg and then the nachos
5. Preheat the air fryer to 180°C
6. Cook for 8 minutes

Crispy Cajun Fish Fingers

Servings: 2
Cooking Time:xx

Ingredients:
- 350 g/12 oz. cod loins
- 1 teaspoon smoked paprika
- ½ teaspoon cayenne pepper
- ½ teaspoon onion granules
- ¾ teaspoon dried oregano
- ¼ teaspoon dried thyme
- ½ teaspoon salt
- ½ teaspoon unrefined sugar
- 40 g/½ cup dried breadcrumbs (gluten-free if you wish, see page 9)
- 2 tablespoons plain/all-purpose flour (gluten-free if you wish)
- 1 egg, beaten

Directions:
1. Slice the cod into 6 equal fish 'fingers'. Mix the spices, herbs, salt and sugar together, then combine with the breadcrumbs. Lay out three bowls: one with flour, one with beaten egg and one with the Cajun-spiced breadcrumbs. Dip each fish finger into the flour, then the egg, then the breadcrumbs until fully coated.
2. Preheat the air-fryer to 180°C/350°F.
3. Add the fish to the preheated air-fryer and air-fry for 6 minutes, until cooked inside. Check the internal temperature of the fish has reached at least 75°C/167°F using a meat thermometer – if not, cook for another few minutes.

Beer Battered Fish Tacos

Servings: 2
Cooking Time:xx

Ingredients:
- 300g cod fillets
- 2 eggs
- 1 can of Mexican beer
- 300g cornstarch
- 300g flour
- 2 soft corn tortillas
- ½ tsp chilli powder
- 1 tbsp cumin
- Salt and pepper to taste

Directions:
1. Whisk together the eggs and beer
2. In a separate bowl whisk together cornstarch, chilli powder, flour, cumin and salt and pepper
3. Coat the fish in the egg mixture then coat in flour mixture
4. Spray the air fryer with non stick spray and add the fish
5. Set your fryer to 170ºC and cook for 15 minutes
6. Place the fish in a corn tortilla

Garlic Butter Salmon

Servings: 2
Cooking Time:xx

Ingredients:
- 2 salmon fillets, boneless with the skin left on
- 1 tsp minced garlic
- 2 tbsp melted butter
- 1 tsp chopped parsley
- Salt and pepper to taste

Directions:
1. Preheat the air fryer to 270 ºC
2. Take a bowl and combine the melted butter, parsley and garlic to create a sauce
3. Season the salmon to your liking
4. Brush the salmon with the garlic mixture, on both sides
5. Place the salmon into the fryer, with the skin side facing down
6. Cook for 10 minutes - the salmon is done when it flakes with ease

Thai Salmon Patties

Servings: 7
Cooking Time:xx

Ingredients:
- 1 large can of salmon, drained and bones removed
- 30g panko breadcrumbs
- ¼ tsp salt
- 1 ½ tbsp Thai red curry paste
- 1 ½ tbsp brown sugar
- Zest of 1 lime
- 2 eggs
- Cooking spray

Directions:
1. Take a large bowl and combine all ingredients together until smooth
2. Use your hands to create patties that are around 1 inch in thickness
3. Preheat your air fryer to 180ºC
4. Coat the patties with cooking spray
5. Cook for 4 minutes each side

Gluten Free Honey And Garlic Shrimp

Servings: 2
Cooking Time:xx

Ingredients:
- 500g fresh shrimp
- 5 tbsp honey
- 2 tbsp gluten free soy sauce
- 2 tbsp tomato ketchup
- 250g frozen stir fry vegetables
- 1 crushed garlic clove
- 1 tsp fresh ginger
- 2 tbsp cornstarch

Directions:
1. Simmer the honey, soy sauce, garlic, tomato ketchup and ginger in a saucepan
2. Add the cornstarch and whisk until sauce thickens
3. Coat the shrimp with the sauce
4. Line the air fryer with foil and add the shrimp and vegetables
5. Cook at 180ºC for 10 minutes

Air Fried Scallops

Servings: 2
Cooking Time:xx

Ingredients:

- 6 scallops
- 1 tbsp olive oil
- Salt and pepper to taste

Directions:

1. Brush the filets with olive oil
2. Sprinkle with salt and pepper
3. Place in the air fryer and cook at 200ºC for 2 mins
4. Turn the scallops over and cook for another 2 minutes

Copycat Fish Fingers

Servings: 2
Cooking Time:xx

Ingredients:

- 2 slices wholemeal bread, grated into breadcrumbs
- 50g plain flour
- 1 beaten egg
- 1 white fish fillet
- The juice of 1 small lemon
- 1 tsp parsley
- 1 tsp thyme
- 1 tsp mixed herbs
- Salt and pepper to taste

Directions:

1. Preheat the air fryer to 180ºC
2. Add salt pepper and parsley to the breadcrumbs and combine well
3. Place the egg in another bowl
4. Place the flour in a separate bowl
5. Place the fish into a food processor and add the lemon juice, salt, pepper thyme and mixed herbs
6. Blitz to create a crumb-like consistency
7. Roll your fish in the flour, then the egg and then the breadcrumbs
8. Cook at 180ºC for 8 minutes

Peppery Lemon Shrimp

Servings: 2
Cooking Time:xx

Ingredients:

- 300g uncooked shrimp
- 1 tbsp olive oil
- 1 the juice of 1 lemon
- 0.25 tsp garlic powder
- 1 sliced lemon
- 1 tsp pepper
- 0.25 tsp paprika

Directions:

1. Heat the fryer to 200ºC
2. Take a medium sized mixing bowl and combine the lemon juice, pepper, garlic powder, paprika and the olive oil together
3. Add the shrimp to the bowl and make sure they're well coated
4. Arrange the shrimp into the basket of the fryer
5. Cook for between 6-8 minutes, until firm and pink

Zesty Fish Fillets

Servings: 2
Cooking Time:xx

Ingredients:

- 30g dry ranch seasoning
- 2 beaten eggs
- 100g breadcrumbs
- 2.5 tbsp vegetable oil
- 4 fish fillets of your choice
- Wedges of lemon to serve

Directions:

1. Preheat the air fryer to 180ºC
2. Mix the bread crumbs and seasoning together add the oil and combine
3. Dip the fish into the egg and then coat in the breadcrumb mix
4. Place in the air fryer and cook for 12 minutes
5. Serve with lemon wedges

Air Fryer Mussels

Servings: 2
Cooking Time:xx

Ingredients:
- 400g mussels
- 1 tbsp butter
- 200ml water
- 1 tsp basil
- 2 tsp minced garlic
- 1 tsp chives
- 1 tsp parsley

Directions:
1. Preheat air fryer to 200ºC
2. Clean the mussels, soak for 30 minutes, and remove the beard
3. Add all ingredients to an air fryer-safe pan
4. Cook for 3 minutes
5. Check to see if the mussels have opened, if not cook for a further 2 minutes. Once all mussels are open, they are ready to eat.

Fish In Foil

Servings: 2
Cooking Time:xx

Ingredients:
- 1 tablespoon avocado oil or olive oil, plus extra for greasing
- 1 tablespoon soy sauce (or tamari)
- 1½ teaspoons freshly grated garlic
- 1½ teaspoons freshly grated ginger
- 1 small red chilli/chile, finely chopped
- 2 skinless, boneless white fish fillets (about 350 g/12 oz. total weight)

Directions:
1. Mix the oil, soy sauce, garlic, ginger and chilli/chile together. Brush a little oil onto two pieces of foil, then lay the fish in the centre of the foil. Spoon the topping mixture over the fish. Wrap the foil around the fish to make a parcel, with a gap above the fish but shallow enough to fit in your air-fryer basket.
2. Preheat the air-fryer to 180ºC/350ºF.
3. Add the foil parcels to the preheated air-fryer and air-fry for 7–10 minutes, depending on the thickness of your fillets. The fish should just flake when a fork is inserted. Serve immediately.

Store-cupboard Fishcakes

Servings: 3
Cooking Time:xx

Ingredients:
- 400 g/14 oz. cooked potato – either mashed potato or the insides of jacket potatoes (see page 124)
- 2 x 150–200-g/5½–7-oz. cans fish, such as tuna or salmon, drained
- 2 eggs
- ¾ teaspoon salt
- 1 teaspoon dried parsley
- ½ teaspoon freshly ground black pepper
- 1 tablespoon olive oil
- caper dressing (see page 79), to serve

Directions:
1. Mix the cooked potato, fish, eggs, salt, parsley and pepper together in a bowl, then divide into 6 equal portions and form into fishcakes. Drizzle the olive oil over both sides of each fishcake.
2. Preheat the air-fryer to 180ºC/350ºF.
3. Add the fishcakes to the preheated air-fryer and air-fry for 15 minutes, turning halfway through cooking. Serve with salad and tartare sauce or Caper Dressing.

Shrimp With Yum Yum Sauce

Servings: 4
Cooking Time:xx

Ingredients:
- 400g peeled jumbo shrimp
- 1 tbsp soy sauce
- 1 tbsp garlic paste
- 1 tbsp ginger paste
- 4 tbsp mayo
- 2 tbsp ketchup
- 1 tbsp sugar
- 1 tsp paprika
- 1 tsp garlic powder

Directions:
1. Mix soy sauce, garlic paste and ginger paste in a bowl. Add the shrimp, allow to marinate for 15 minutes
2. In another bowl mix ketchup, mayo, sugar, paprika and the garlic powder to make the yum yum sauce.
3. Set the air fryer to 200ºC, place shrimp in the basket and cook for 8-10 minutes

Desserts Recipes

Desserts Recipes

Special Oreos

Servings: 9
Cooking Time:xx

Ingredients:
- 100g pancake mix
- 25ml water
- Cooking spray
- 9 Oreos
- 1 tbsp icing sugar

Directions:
1. Mix pancake mix and water until well combined
2. Line the air fryer with parchment paper and spray with cooking spray
3. Preheat the air fryer to 200°C
4. Dip each cookie in the pancake mix and place in the air fryer
5. Cook for 5 minutes, turn and cook for a further 3 minutes
6. Sprinkle with icing sugar to serve

Strawberry Lemonade Pop Tarts

Servings: 12
Cooking Time:xx

Ingredients:
- 300g whole wheat flour
- 225g white flour
- ¼ tsp salt
- 2 tbsp light brown sugar
- 300g icing sugar
- 2 tbsp lemon juice
- Zest of 1 lemon
- 150g cold coconut oil
- 1 tsp vanilla extract
- 75ml ice cold water
- Strawberry Jam
- 1 tsp melted coconut oil
- ¼ tsp vanilla extract
- Sprinkles

Directions:
1. In a bowl mix the flours, salt and sugar. Mix in the cold coconut oil
2. Add 1 tsp vanilla and 1 tbsp at a time of the ice cold water, mix until a dough is formed
3. Take the dough and roll out thinly on a floured surface. Cut into 5cm by 7cm rectangles
4. Place a tsp of jam in the centre of half the rectangles, wet the edges place another rectangle on the top and seal
5. Place in the air fryer and cook at 200°C for 10 minutes. Allow to cool
6. Mix the icing sugar, coconut oil, lemon juice and lemon zest in a bowl. Mix well. Top the pop tarts and add sprinkles to serve

Profiteroles

Servings: 9
Cooking Time:xx

Ingredients:
- 100g butter
- 200g plain flour
- 6 eggs
- 300ml water
- 2 tsp vanilla extract
- 300ml whipped cream
- 100g milk chocolate
- 2 tbsp whipped cream
- 50g butter
- 2 tsp icing sugar

Directions:
1. Preheat the air fryer to 170°C
2. Place the butter and water in a pan over a medium heat, bring to the boil, remove from the heat and stir in the flour
3. Return to the heat stirring until a dough is formed
4. Mix in the eggs and stir until mixture is smooth, make into profiterole shapes and cook in the air fryer for 10 minutes
5. For the filling whisk together 300ml whipped cream, vanilla extract and the icing sugar
6. For the topping place the butter, 2tbsp whipped cream and chocolate in a bowl and melt over a pan of hot water until mixed together
7. Pipe the filling into the roles and finish off with a chocolate topping

Chocolate Mug Cake

Servings: 1
Cooking Time:xx

Ingredients:
- 30g self raising flour
- 5 tbsp sugar
- 1 tbsp cocoa powder
- 3 tbsp milk
- 3 tsp coconut oil

Directions:
1. Mix all the ingredients together in a mug
2. Heat the air fryer to 200ºC
3. Place the mug in the air fryer and cook for 10 minutes

Lemon Tarts

Servings: 8
Cooking Time:xx

Ingredients:
- 100g butter
- 225g plain flour
- 30g caster sugar
- Zest and juice of 1 lemon
- 4 tsp lemon curd

Directions:
1. In a bowl mix together butter, flour and sugar until it forms crumbs, add the lemon zest and juice
2. Add a little water at a time and mix to form a dough
3. Roll out the dough and line 8 small ramekins with it
4. Add ¼ tsp of lemon curd to each ramekin
5. Cook in the air fryer for 15 minutes at 180ºC

Banana Maple Flapjack

Servings:9
Cooking Time:xx

Ingredients:
- 100 g/7 tablespoons butter (or plant-based spread if you wish)
- 75 g/5 tablespoons maple syrup
- 2 ripe bananas, mashed well with the back of a fork
- 1 teaspoon vanilla extract
- 240 g/2½ cups rolled oats/quick-cooking oats

Directions:
1. Gently heat the butter and maple syrup in a medium saucepan over a low heat until melted. Stir in the mashed banana, vanilla and oats and combine all ingredients. Pour the flapjack mixture into a 15 x 15-cm/6 x 6-in. baking pan and cover with foil.
2. Preheat the air-fryer to 200ºC/400ºF.
3. Add the baking pan to the preheated air-fryer and air-fry for 12 minutes, then remove the foil and cook for a further 4 minutes to brown the top. Leave to cool before cutting into 9 squares.

Banana Bread

Servings: 8
Cooking Time:xx

Ingredients:
- 200g flour
- 1 tsp cinnamon
- ½ tsp salt
- ¼ tsp baking soda
- 2 ripe banana mashed
- 2 large eggs
- 75g sugar
- 25g plain yogurt
- 2 tbsp oil
- 1 tsp vanilla extract
- 2 tbsp chopped walnuts
- Cooking spray

Directions:
1. Line a 6 inch cake tin with parchment paper and coat with cooking spray
2. Whisk together flour, cinnamon, salt and baking soda set aside
3. In another bowl mix together remaining ingredients, add the flour mix and combine well
4. Pour batter into the cake tin and place in the air fryer
5. Cook at 155ºC for 35 minutes turning halfway through

Lava Cakes

Servings: 4
Cooking Time:xx

Ingredients:
- 1 ½ tbsp self raising flour
- 3 ½ tbsp sugar
- 150g butter
- 150g dark chocolate, chopped
- 2 eggs

Directions:
1. Preheat the air fryer to 175ºC
2. Grease 4 ramekin dishes
3. Melt chocolate and butter in the microwave for about 3 minutes
4. Whisk the eggs and sugar together until pale and frothy
5. Pour melted chocolate into the eggs and stir in the flour
6. Fill the ramekins ¾ full, place in the air fryer and cook for 10 minutes

Fruit Scones

Servings: 4
Cooking Time:xx

Ingredients:
- 225g self raising flour
- 50g butter
- 50g sultanas
- 25g caster sugar
- 1 egg
- A little milk

Directions:
1. Place the flour in a bowl and rub in the butter, add the sultanas and mix
2. Stir in the caster sugar
3. Add the egg and mix well
4. Add a little bit of milk at a time to form a dough
5. Shape the dough into scones
6. Place in the air fryer and bake at 180ºC for 8 minutes

Peanut Butter & Chocolate Baked Oats

Servings:9
Cooking Time:xx

Ingredients:
- 150 g/1 heaped cup rolled oats/quick-cooking oats
- 50 g/⅓ cup dark chocolate chips or buttons
- 300 ml/1¼ cups milk or plant-based milk
- 50 g/3½ tablespoons Greek or plant-based yogurt
- 1 tablespoon runny honey or maple syrup
- ½ teaspoon ground cinnamon or ground ginger
- 65 g/scant ⅓ cup smooth peanut butter

Directions:
1. Stir all the ingredients together in a bowl, then transfer to a baking dish that fits your air-fryer drawer.
2. Preheat the air-fryer to 180ºC/350ºF.
3. Add the baking dish to the preheated air-fryer and air-fry for 10 minutes. Remove from the air-fryer and serve hot, cut into 9 squares.

Oat-covered Banana Fritters

Servings: 4
Cooking Time:xx

Ingredients:
- 3 tablespoons plain/all-purpose flour (gluten-free if you wish)
- 1 egg, beaten
- 90 g/3 oz. oatcakes (gluten-free if you wish) or oat-based cookies, crushed to a crumb consistency
- 1½ teaspoons ground cinnamon
- 1 tablespoon unrefined sugar
- 4 bananas, peeled

Directions:
1. Preheat the air-fryer to 180ºC/350ºF.
2. Set up three bowls – one with flour, one with beaten egg and the other with the oatcake crumb, cinnamon and sugar mixed together. Coat the bananas in flour, then in egg, then in the crumb mixture.
3. Add the bananas to the preheated air-fryer and air-fry for 10 minutes. Serve warm.

Cherry Pies

Servings: 6
Cooking Time:xx

Ingredients:
- 300g prepared shortcrust pastry
- 75g cherry pie filling
- Cooking spray
- 3 tbsp icing sugar
- ½ tsp milk

Directions:
1. Cut out 6 pies with a cookie cutter
2. Add 1 ½ tbsp filling to each pie
3. Fold the dough in half and seal around the edges with a fork
4. Place in the air fryer, spray with cooking spray
5. Cook at 175ºC for 10 minutes
6. Mix icing sugar and milk and drizzled over cooled pies to serve

Melting Moments

Servings: 9
Cooking Time:xx

Ingredients:
- 100g butter
- 75g caster sugar
- 150g self raising flour
- 1 egg
- 50g white chocolate
- 3 tbsp desiccated coconut
- 1 tsp vanilla essence

Directions:
1. Preheat the air fryer to 180ºC
2. Cream together the butter and sugar, beat in the egg and vanilla
3. Bash the white chocolate into small pieces
4. Add the flour and chocolate and mix well
5. Roll into 9 small balls and cover in coconut
6. Place in the air fryer and cook for 8 minutes and a further 6 minutes at 160ºC

Pecan & Molasses Flapjack

Servings:9
Cooking Time:xx

Ingredients:
- 120 g/½ cup plus 2 teaspoons butter or plant-based spread, plus extra for greasing
- 40 g/2 tablespoons blackstrap molasses
- 60 g/5 tablespoons unrefined sugar
- 50 g/½ cup chopped pecans
- 200 g/1½ cups porridge oats/steelcut oats (not rolled or jumbo)

Directions:
1. Preheat the air-fryer to 180ºC/350ºF.
2. Grease and line a 15 x 15-cm/6 x 6-in. baking pan.
3. In a large saucepan melt the butter/spread, molasses and sugar. Once melted, stir in the pecans, then the oats. As soon as they are combined, tip the mixture into the prepared baking pan and cover with foil.
4. Place the foil-covered baking pan in the preheated air-fryer and air-fry for 10 minutes. Remove the foil, then cook for a further 2 minutes to brown the top. Leave to cool, then cut into 9 squares.

Thai Style Bananas

Servings: 4
Cooking Time:xx

Ingredients:
- 4 ripe bananas
- 2 tbsp flour
- 2 tbsp rice flour
- 2 tbsp corn flour
- 2 tbsp desiccated coconut
- Pinch salt
- ½ tsp baking powder
- Sesame seeds

Directions:
1. Add all the ingredients to a bowl apart from the sesame seeds mix well
2. Line the air fryer with foil
3. Dip the banana into the batter mix then roll in the sesame seeds
4. Place in the air fryer and cook for about 15 minutes at 200ºC turning halfway

Pumpkin Spiced Bread Pudding

Servings: 2
Cooking Time:xx

Ingredients:

- 175g heavy cream
- 500g pumpkin puree
- 30ml milk
- 25g sugar
- 1 large egg, plus one extra yolk
- ⅛ tsp salt
- ½ tsp pumpkin spice
- 500g cubed crusty bread
- 4 tbsp butter

Directions:

1. Place all of the ingredients apart from the bread and butter into a bowl and mix.
2. Add the bread and melted butter to the bowl and mix well
3. Heat the air fryer to 175ºC
4. Pour the mix into a baking tin and cook in the air fryer for 35-40 minutes
5. Serve with maple cream

Cinnamon-maple Pineapple Kebabs

Servings: 2
Cooking Time:xx

Ingredients:

- 4 x pineapple strips, roughly 2 x 2 cm/¾ x ¾ in. by length of pineapple
- 1 teaspoon maple syrup
- ½ teaspoon vanilla extract
- ¼ teaspoon ground cinnamon
- Greek or plant-based yogurt and grated lime zest, to serve

Directions:

1. Line the air-fryer with an air-fryer liner or a piece of pierced parchment paper. Preheat the air-fryer to 180ºC/350ºF.
2. Stick small metal skewers through the pineapple lengthways. Mix the maple syrup and vanilla extract together, then drizzle over the pineapple and sprinkle over the cinnamon.
3. Add the skewers to the preheated lined air-fryer and air-fry for 15 minutes, turning once. If there is any maple-vanilla mixture left after the initial drizzle, then drizzle this over the pineapple during cooking too. Serve with yogurt and lime zest.

Breakfast Muffins

Servings:4
Cooking Time:xx

Ingredients:

- 1 eating apple, cored and grated
- 40 g/2 heaped tablespoons maple syrup
- 40 ml/3 tablespoons oil (avocado, olive or coconut), plus extra for greasing
- 1 egg
- 40 ml/3 tablespoons milk (plant-based if you wish)
- 90 g/scant ¾ cup brown rice flour
- 50 g/½ cup ground almonds
- ¾ teaspoon ground cinnamon
- ⅛ teaspoon ground cloves
- ¼ teaspoon salt
- 1 teaspoon baking powder
- Greek or plant-based yogurt and fresh fruit, to serve

Directions:

1. In a bowl mix the grated apple, maple syrup, oil, egg and milk. In another bowl mix the rice flour, ground almonds, cinnamon, cloves, salt and baking powder. Combine the wet ingredients with the dry, mixing until there are no visible patches of the flour mixture left. Grease 4 ramekins and divide the batter equally between them.
2. Preheat the air-fryer to 160ºC/325ºF.
3. Add the ramekins to the preheated air-fryer and air-fry for 12 minutes. Check the muffins are cooked by inserting a cocktail stick/toothpick into the middle of one of the muffins. If it comes out clean, the muffins are ready; if not, cook for a further couple of minutes.
4. Allow to cool in the ramekins, then remove and serve with your choice of yogurt and fresh fruit.

White Chocolate And Raspberry Loaf

Servings:8
Cooking Time:1 Hour 10 Minutes

Ingredients:

- 400 g / 14 oz plain flour
- 2 tsp baking powder
- 1 tsp ground cinnamon
- ½ tsp salt
- 3 eggs, beaten
- 50 g / 3.5 oz granulated sugar
- 50 g / 3.5 oz brown sugar
- 100 g / 3.5 oz white chocolate chips
- 100 g / 3.5 oz fresh raspberries
- 1 tbsp cocoa powder
- 4 tbsp milk
- 1 tsp vanilla extract

Directions:

1. Preheat the air fryer to 150 °C / 300 °F and line a loaf tin with parchment paper.
2. Combine the plain flour, baking powder, ground cinnamon, and salt in a large mixing bowl.
3. Whisk eggs into the bowl, then stir in the granulated sugar and brown sugar. Mix well before folding in the white chocolate chips, fresh raspberries, cocoa powder, milk, and vanilla extract.
4. Stir the mixture until it is lump-free and transfer into a lined loaf tin. Place the loaf tin into the lined air fryer basket, close the lid, and cook for 30-40 minutes.
5. The cake should be golden and set by the end of the cooking process. Insert a knife into the centre of the cake. It should come out dry when the cake is fully cooked.
6. Remove the cake from the air fryer, still in the loaf tin. Set aside to cool on a drying rack for 20-30 minutes before cutting into slices and serving.

Spiced Apples

Servings: 4
Cooking Time:xx

Ingredients:

- 4 apples, sliced
- 2 tbsp ghee
- 2 tbsp sugar
- 1 tsp apple pie spice

Directions:

1. Place apples in a bowl, add the ghee and sprinkle with sugar and apple pie spice

2. Place in a tin that will fit the air fryer
3. Heat the air fryer to 175°C
4. Put the tin in the air fryer and cook for 10 minutes until tender

French Toast Sticks

Servings: 12
Cooking Time:xx

Ingredients:

- 2 eggs
- 25g milk
- 1 tbsp melted butter
- 1 tsp vanilla extract
- 1 tsp cinnamon
- 4 slices bread, cut into thirds
- 1 tsp icing sugar

Directions:

1. Mix eggs, milk, butter, vanilla and cinnamon together in a bowl
2. Line the air fryer with parchment paper
3. Dip each piece of bread into the egg mixture
4. Place in the air fryer and cook at 190°C for 6 minutes, turn over and cook for another 3 minutes
5. Sprinkle with icing sugar to serve

Lemon Pies

Servings: 6
Cooking Time:xx

Ingredients:

- 1 pack of pastry
- 1 egg beaten
- 200g lemon curd
- 225g powdered sugar
- ½ lemon

Directions:

1. Preheat the air fryer to 180°C
2. Cut out 6 circles from the pastry using a cookie cutter
3. Add 1 tbsp of lemon curd to each circle, brush the edges with egg and fold over
4. Press around the edges of the dough with a fork to seal
5. Brush the pies with the egg and cook in the air fryer for 10 minutes
6. Mix the lemon juice with the powdered sugar to make the icing and drizzle on the cooked pies

Birthday Cheesecake

Servings: 8
Cooking Time:xx

Ingredients:
- 6 Digestive biscuits
- 50g melted butter
- 800g soft cheese
- 500g caster sugar
- 4 tbsp cocoa powder
- 6 eggs
- 2 tbsp honey
- 1 tbsp vanilla

Directions:
1. Flour a spring form tin to prevent sticking
2. Crush the biscuits and then mix with the melted butter, press into the bottom and sides of the tin
3. Mix the caster sugar and soft cheese with an electric mixer. Add 5 eggs, honey and vanilla. Mix well
4. Spoon half the mix into the pan and pat down well. Place in the air fryer and cook at 180°C for 20 minutes then 160°C for 15 minutes and then 150°C for 20 minutes
5. Mix the cocoa and the last egg into the remaining mix. Spoon over the over the bottom layer and place in the fridge. Chill for 11 hours

Milk And White Chocolate Chip Air Fryer Donuts With Frosting

Servings:4
Cooking Time:10 Minutes

Ingredients:
- For the donuts:
- 200 ml milk (any kind)
- 50 g / 3.5 oz brown sugar
- 50 g / 3.5 oz granulated sugar
- 1 tbsp active dry yeast
- 2 tbsp olive oil
- 4 tbsp butter, melted
- 1 egg, beaten
- 1 tsp vanilla extract
- 400 g / 14 oz plain flour
- 4 tbsp cocoa powder
- 100 g / 3.5 oz milk chocolate chips
- For the frosting:
- 5 tbsp powdered sugar
- 2 tbsp cocoa powder
- 100 ml heavy cream
- 50 g / 1.8 oz white chocolate chips, melted

Directions:
1. To make the donuts, whisk together the milk, brown and granulated sugars, and active dry yeast in a bowl. Set aside for a few minutes while the yeast starts to get foamy.
2. Stir the melted butter, beaten egg, and vanilla extract into the bowl. Mix well until all of the ingredients are combined.
3. Fold in the plain flour and cocoa powder until a smooth mixture forms.
4. Lightly flour a clean kitchen top surface and roll the dough out. Gently knead the dough for 2-3 minutes until it becomes soft and slightly tacky.
5. Transfer the dough into a large mixing bowl and cover it with a clean tea towel or some tinfoil. Leave the dough to rise for around one hour in a warm place.
6. Remove the tea towel or tinfoil from the bowl and roll it out on a floured surface once again. Use a rolling pin to roll the dough into a one-inch thick circle.
7. Use a round cookie cutter to create circular donuts and place each one into a lined air fryer basket.
8. Once all of the donuts have been placed into the air fryer, turn the machine onto 150 °C / 300 °F and close the lid.
9. Cook the donuts for 8-10 minutes until they are slightly golden and crispy on the outside.
10. While the donuts are cooking in the air fryer, make the frosting by combining the powdered sugar, cocoa powder, heavy cream, and melted white chocolate chips in a bowl. Mix well until a smooth, sticky mixture forms.
11. When the donuts are cooked, remove them from the air fryer and set aside to cool for 5-10 minutes. Once cooled, evenly spread some frosting on the top layer of each one. Place in the fridge to set for at least one hour.
12. Enjoy the donuts hot or cold.

Granola

Servings: 3
Cooking Time:xx

Ingredients:
- 60 g/¼ cup runny honey
- 50 g/3 tablespoons coconut oil
- 1 teaspoon vanilla extract
- 100 g/¾ cup jumbo rolled oats/old-fashioned oats (not porridge oats)
- 50 g/½ cup chopped walnuts
- 1 teaspoon ground cinnamon

Directions:
1. Preheat the air-fryer to 180ºC/350ºF.
2. Place the honey, coconut oil and vanilla extract in a small dish. Add this to the preheated air-fryer for 1 minute to melt.
3. In a small bowl combine the oats, nuts and cinnamon. Add the melted honey mixture and toss well, ensuring all the oats and nuts are well coated.
4. Lay an air-fryer liner or a pierced piece of parchment paper on the base of the air-fryer drawer. Add the granola mix on top, spread evenly in one layer. Air-fry for 4 minutes, then stir before cooking for a further 3 minutes. Leave to cool completely before serving or storing in a jar.

Sugar Dough Dippers

Servings: 12
Cooking Time:xx

Ingredients:
- 300g bread dough
- 75g melted butter
- 100g sugar
- 200ml double cream
- 200g semi sweet chocolate
- 2 tbsp amaretto

Directions:
1. Roll the dough into 2 15inch logs, cut each one into 20 slices. Cut each slice in half and twist together 2-3 times. Brush with melted butter and sprinkle with sugar
2. Preheat the air fryer to 150ºC
3. Place dough in the air fryer and cook for 5 minutes, turnover and cook for a further 3 minutes
4. Place the cream in a pan and bring to simmer over a medium heat, place the chocolate chips in a bowl and pour over the cream

5. Mix until the chocolate is melted then stir in the amaretto
6. Serve the dough dippers with the chocolate dip

Fruit Crumble

Servings: 2
Cooking Time:xx

Ingredients:
- 1 diced apple
- 75g frozen blackberries
- 25g brown rice flour
- 2 tbsp sugar
- ½ tsp cinnamon
- 2 tbsp butter

Directions:
1. Preheat air fryer to 150ºC
2. Mix apple and blackberries in an air fryer safe baking pan
3. In a bowl mix the flour, sugar, cinnamon and butter, spoon over the fruit
4. Cook for 15 minutes

Peach Pies

Servings: 8
Cooking Time:xx

Ingredients:
- 2 peaches, peeled and chopped
- 1 tbsp lemon juice
- 3 tbsp sugar
- 1 tsp vanilla extract
- ¼ tsp salt
- 1 tsp cornstarch
- 1 pack ready made pastry
- Cooking spray

Directions:
1. Mix together peaches, lemon juice, sugar and vanilla in a bowl. Stand for 15 minutes
2. Drain the peaches keeping 1 tbsp of the liquid, mix cornstarch into the peaches
3. Cut the pastry into 8 circles, fill with the peach mix
4. Brush the edges of the pastry with water and fold over to form half moons, crimp the edges to seal
5. Coat with cooking spray
6. Add to the air fryer and cook at 170ºC for 12 minutes until golden brown

Grain-free Millionaire's Shortbread

Servings:9
Cooking Time:xx

Ingredients:
- BASE
- 60 g/5 tablespoons coconut oil
- 1 tablespoon maple syrup
- ½ teaspoon vanilla extract
- 180 g/1¼ cups ground almonds
- a pinch of salt
- MIDDLE
- 185 g/1⅓ cups dried pitted dates (soak in hot water for at least 20 minutes, then drain)
- 2 tablespoons almond butter
- 90 g/scant ½ cup canned coconut milk (the thick part once it has separated is ideal)
- TOPPING
- 125 g/½ cup coconut oil
- 4 tablespoons cacao powder
- 1 tablespoon maple syrup

Directions:
1. Preheat the air-fryer to 180ºC/350ºF.
2. To make the base, in a small saucepan melt the coconut oil with the maple syrup and vanilla extract. As soon as the coconut oil is melted, stir in the almonds and the salt off the heat. Press this mixture into a 15 x 15-cm/6 x 6-in. baking pan.
3. Add the baking pan to the preheated air-fryer and cook for 4 minutes, until golden brown on top. Remove from the air-fryer and allow to cool.
4. In a food processor, combine the rehydrated drained dates, almond butter and coconut milk. Once the base is cool, pour this mixture over the base and pop into the freezer to set for an hour.
5. After the base has had 45 minutes in the freezer, make the topping by heating the coconut oil in a saucepan until melted, then whisk in the cacao powder and maple syrup off the heat to make a chocolate syrup. Leave this to cool for 15 minutes, then pour over the set middle layer and return to the freezer for 30 minutes. Cut into 9 squares to serve.

Apple Chips With Yogurt Dip

Servings: 4
Cooking Time:xx

Ingredients:
- 1 apple
- 1 tsp cinnamon
- 2 tsp oil
- Cooking spray
- 25g greek yogurt
- 1 tbsp almond butter
- 1 tsp honey

Directions:
1. Thinly slice the apple, place in a bowl and coat with cinnamon and oil
2. Coat the air fryer with cooking spray and add the apple slices
3. Cook the slices for 12 minutes at 180ºC
4. Mix the butter, honey and yogurt together and serve with the apple slices as a dip

Chocolate Eclairs

Servings: 9
Cooking Time:xx

Ingredients:
- 100g plain flour
- 50g butter
- 3 eggs
- 150ml water
- 25g butter
- 1 tsp vanilla extract
- 1 tsp icing sugar
- 150ml whipped cream
- 50g milk chocolate
- 1 tbsp whipped cream

Directions:
1. Preheat the air fryer to 180ºC
2. Add 50g of butter to a pan along with the water and melt over a medium heat
3. Remove from the heat and stir in the flour. Return to the heat until mix form a single ball of dough
4. Allow to cool, once cool beat in the eggs until you have a smooth dough
5. Make into eclair shapes, cook in the air fryer at 180ºC for 10 minutes and then 160ºC for 8 minutes
6. Mix the vanilla, icing sugar and 150ml of whipping cream until nice and thick
7. Once cool fill each eclair with the cream mix
8. Place the chocolate, 1 tbsp whipped cream and 25g of butter in a glass bowl and melt over a pan of boiling water. Top the eclairs

Recipe for:

Ingredients:

Equipment:

Description:

Instructions:

Date: _____

MY SHOPPING LIST

APPENDIX A: Measurement Conversions

BASIC KITCHEN CONVERSIONS & EQUIVALENTS

DRY MEASUREMENTS CONVERSION CHART

3 TEASPOONS = 1 TABLESPOON = 1/16 CUP

6 TEASPOONS = 2 TABLESPOONS = 1/8 CUP

12 TEASPOONS = 4 TABLESPOONS = 1/4 CUP

24 TEASPOONS = 8 TABLESPOONS = 1/2 CUP

36 TEASPOONS = 12 TABLESPOONS = 3/4 CUP

48 TEASPOONS = 16 TABLESPOONS = 1 CUP

METRIC TO US COOKING CONVERSIONS

OVEN TEMPERATURES

120 °C = 250 °F

160 °C = 320 °F

180° C = 350 °F

205 °C = 400 °F

220 °C = 425 °F

LIQUID MEASUREMENTS CONVERSION CHART

8 FLUID OUNCES = 1 CUP = 1/2 PINT = 1/4 QUART

16 FLUID OUNCES = 2 CUPS = 1 PINT = 1/2 QUART

32 FLUID OUNCES = 4 CUPS = 2 PINTS = 1 QUART
 = 1/4 GALLON

128 FLUID OUNCES = 16 CUPS = 8 PINTS = 4 QUARTS = 1 GALLON

BAKING IN GRAMS

1 CUP FLOUR = 140 GRAMS

1 CUP SUGAR = 150 GRAMS

1 CUP POWDERED SUGAR = 160 GRAMS

1 CUP HEAVY CREAM = 235 GRAMS

VOLUME

1 MILLILITER = 1/5 TEASPOON

5 ML = 1 TEASPOON

15 ML = 1 TABLESPOON

240 ML = 1 CUP OR 8 FLUID OUNCES

1 LITER = 34 FL. OUNCES

US TO METRIC COOKING CONVERSIONS

1/5 TSP = 1 ML

1 TSP = 5 ML

1 TBSP = 15 ML

1 FL OUNCE = 30 ML

1 CUP = 237 ML

1 PINT (2 CUPS) = 473 ML

1 QUART (4 CUPS) = .95 LITER

1 GALLON (16 CUPS) = 3.8 LITERS

1 OZ = 28 GRAMS

1 POUND = 454 GRAMS

BUTTER

1 CUP BUTTER = 2 STICKS = 8 OUNCES = 230 GRAMS = 8 TABLESPOONS

WHAT DOES 1 CUP EQUAL

1 CUP = 8 FLUID OUNCES

1 CUP = 16 TABLESPOONS

1 CUP = 48 TEASPOONS

1 CUP = 1/2 PINT

1 CUP = 1/4 QUART

1 CUP = 1/16 GALLON

1 CUP = 240 ML

WEIGHT

1 GRAM = .035 OUNCES

100 GRAMS = 3.5 OUNCES

500 GRAMS = 1.1 POUNDS

1 KILOGRAM = 35 OUNCES

BAKING PAN CONVERSIONS

1 CUP ALL-PURPOSE FLOUR = 4.5 OZ

1 CUP ROLLED OATS = 3 OZ 1 LARGE EGG = 1.7 OZ

1 CUP BUTTER = 8 OZ 1 CUP MILK = 8 OZ

1 CUP HEAVY CREAM = 8.4 OZ

1 CUP GRANULATED SUGAR = 7.1 OZ

1 CUP PACKED BROWN SUGAR = 7.75 OZ

1 CUP VEGETABLE OIL = 7.7 OZ

1 CUP UNSIFTED POWDERED SUGAR = 4.4 OZ

BAKING PAN CONVERSIONS

9-INCH ROUND CAKE PAN = 12 CUPS

10-INCH TUBE PAN = 16 CUPS

11-INCH BUNDT PAN = 12 CUPS

9-INCH SPRINGFORM PAN = 10 CUPS

9 X 5 INCH LOAF PAN = 8 CUPS

9-INCH SQUARE PAN = 8 CUPS

Appendix B : Recipes Index

A

Air Fried Scallops   73
Air Fryer Bbq Chicken   53
Air Fryer Cheese Sandwich   33
Air Fryer Chicken Thigh Schnitzel   52
Air Fryer Corn On The Cob   44
Air Fryer Eggy Bread   43
Air Fryer Mussels   74
Air Fryer Sesame Chicken Thighs   55
Air-fried Artichoke Hearts   33
Air-fried Pickles   23
Alternative Stuffed Potatoes   40
Apple Chips With Yogurt Dip   84
Artichoke Pasta   36
Asian Devilled Eggs   26
Asparagus & Steak Parcels   58
Aubergine Parmesan   39
Avocado Fries   16

B

Bacon Smokies   23
Bacon Wrapped Chicken Thighs   50
Baked Feta, Tomato & Garlic Pasta   34
Baked Panko Cod   70
Banana Bread   77
Banana Maple Flapjack   77
Bbq Chicken Tenders   56
Beef Kebobs   64
Beef Nacho Pinwheels   65
Beer Battered Fish Tacos   72
Beetroot Crisps   20
Birthday Cheesecake   82
Blanket Breakfast Eggs   18
Blueberry & Lemon Breakfast Muffins   13
Blueberry Bread   18
Bocconcini Balls   17
Breaded Pork Chops   58
Breakfast Eggs & Spinach   12
Breakfast Muffins   80
Breakfast Sausage Burgers   18

Buffalo Cauliflower Bites   37
Buffalo Chicken Wontons   55
Buffalo Wings   53
Buttermilk Chicken   51
Buttermilk Pork Chops   62
Butternut Squash   39

C

Cajun Shrimp Boil   69
Carne Asada Chips   63
Carrot & Parmesan Chips   40
Cauliflower With Hot Sauce And Blue Cheese Sauce   42
Char Siu Buffalo   61
Charred Chicken Breasts   52
Cheese & Ham Sliders   60
Cheese Wontons   25
Cheesy Broccoli   45
Cheesy Garlic Asparagus   44
Cheesy Meatballs   59
Cheesy Sausage Breakfast Pockets   17
Cherry Pies   79
Chicken & Potatoes   49
Chicken And Cheese Chimichangas   51
Chicken And Wheat Stir Fry   49
Chicken Balls, Greek-style   51
Chicken Fried Rice   56
Chicken Jalfrezi   55
Chicken Kiev   55
Chicken Milanese   56
Chicken Tikka   54
Chicken Tikka Masala   48
Chickpea And Sweetcorn Falafel   32
Chilli Lime Tilapia   67
Chinese Pork With Pineapple   62
Chocolate Eclairs   84
Chocolate Mug Cake   77
Cinnamon-maple Pineapple Kebabs   80
Coconut Shrimp   70
Cod Nuggets   68
Copycat Burger   63
Copycat Fish Fingers   73
Corn On The Cob   41
Cornflake Chicken Nuggets   53
Courgette Burgers   30
Courgette Fries   12
Courgette Meatballs   31

Crispy Cajun Fish Fingers   71
Crispy Cinnamon French Toast   46
Crispy Cornish Hen   51
Crispy Nacho Prawns   71
Crunchy Mexican Breakfast Wrap   15
Cumin Shoestring Carrots   14

D

Delicious Breakfast Casserole   14

E

Easy Air Fryer Sausage   11
Easy Cheese & Bacon Toasties   14
Easy Cheesy Scrambled Eggs   16
Easy Omelette   18
Egg & Bacon Breakfast Cups   17
Egg Fried Rice   39

F

Falafel Burgers   35
Fish In Foil   74
Fish Sticks With Tartar Sauce Batter   69
French Toast   15
French Toast Sticks   81
Fruit Crumble   83
Fruit Scones   78

G

Garlic And Parsley Potatoes   45
Garlic Butter Salmon   72
Garlic Cheese Bread   21
Garlic Tilapia   70
Gluten Free Honey And Garlic Shrimp   72
Goat's Cheese Tartlets   35
Grain-free Chicken Katsu   54
Grain-free Millionaire's Shortbread   84
Granola   83
Grilled Bacon And Cheese   43

H

Hamburgers   58
Hamburgers With Feta   61
Hard Boiled Eggs Air Fryer Style   11
Healthy Bang Bang Chicken   50
Healthy Stuffed Peppers   16
Homemade Crispy Pepperoni Pizza   65
Honey Cajun Chicken Thighs   53
Honey Roasted Parsnips   45

I

Italian Meatballs   59

J

Jackfruit Taquitos   37
Jalapeño Pockets   26
Jalapeño Poppers   21
Jamaican Jerk Pork   60
Japanese Pork Chops   59

K

Korean Chicken Wings   22

L

Lava Cakes   78
Lemon Pepper Shrimp   69
Lemon Pies   81
Lemon Tarts   77
Lentil Balls With Zingy Rice   35
Loaded Hash Browns   13
Lobster Tails   68
Lumpia   21

M

Mac & Cheese Bites   22
Maine Seafood   68
Mediterranean Vegetables   41
Melting Moments   79
Mexican Breakfast Burritos   16

Mexican Rice   42
Milk And White Chocolate Chip Air Fryer Donuts With Frosting   82
Miso Mushrooms On Sourdough Toast   36
Monte Cristo Breakfast Sandwich   15
Morning Sausage Wraps   14
Mozzarella Sticks   24
Mushrooms Stuffed With Crab   67
Mustard Glazed Pork   61

O

Oat & Parmesan Crusted Fish Fillets   69
Oat-covered Banana Fritters   78
Olive Stained Turkey Breast   49
Onion Bahji   23
Onion Dumplings   30
Onion Pakoda   25
Oozing Baked Eggs   13
Orange Sesame Cauliflower   42
Orange Tofu   41

P

Pakoras   29
Pao De Queijo   21
Pasta Chips   27
Peach Pies   83
Peanut Butter & Chocolate Baked Oats   78
Pecan & Molasses Flapjack   79
Pepper & Lemon Chicken Wings   52
Pepperoni Bread   25
Peppers With Aioli Dip   24
Peppery Lemon Shrimp   73
Pitta Pizza   17
Pizza Chicken Nuggets   50
Pizza Dogs   62
Polenta Fries   12
Popcorn Tofu   22
Pork Chilli Cheese Dogs   61
Pork Chops With Raspberry And Balsamic   64
Pork Jerky   24
Pork Schnitzel   63
Pork Taquitos   61
Potato Fries   13
Potato Gratin   29
Potato Hay   43

Potato Wedges With Rosemary   44
Pretzel Bites   27
Profiteroles   76
Pumpkin Spiced Bread Pudding   80

R

Radish Hash Browns   36
Ranch Style Fish Fillets   68
Ratatouille   33
Ricotta Stuffed Aubergine   46
Roast Beef   63
Roast Pork   64
Roasted Cauliflower   32
Roasted Okra   44
Roasted Vegetable Pasta   29

S

Salt And Vinegar Chickpeas   23
Salt And Vinegar Chips   26
Shakshuka   31
Shrimp With Yum Yum Sauce   74
Shrimp Wrapped With Bacon   71
Smoky Chicken Breast   48
Snack Style Falafel   20
Spanakopita Bites   37
Special Oreos   76
Spiced Apples   81
Spicy Peanuts   24
Spicy Spanish Potatoes   34
Spring Ratatouille   30
Spring Rolls   20
Steak Dinner   62
Steak Fajitas   64
Steak Popcorn Bites   65
Sticky Chicken Tikka Drumsticks   48
Store-cupboard Fishcakes   74
Strawberry Lemonade Pop Tarts   76
Stuffed Mushrooms   26
Sugar Dough Dippers   83
Super Easy Fries   40
Swede Fries   11
Sweet & Spicy Baby Peppers   46
Sweet And Sticky Parsnips And Carrots   44
Sweet And Sticky Ribs   60

Sweet Potato Crisps   20
Sweet Potato Taquitos   34
Sweet Potato Tots   39
Sweet Potato Wedges   45

T

Tahini Beef Bites   60
Tempura Veggies   33
Tex Mex Hash Browns   41
Thai Bites   27
Thai Fish Cakes   67
Thai Salmon Patties   72
Thai Style Bananas   79
Tilapia Fillets   71
Tofu Bowls   32
Tortellini Bites   22
Tostones   25
Traditional Empanadas   58
Traditional Fish And Chips   70
Turkey And Mushroom Burgers   52

V

Vegan Fried Ravioli   30
Vegan Meatballs   31
Veggie Bakes   34

W

White Chocolate And Raspberry Loaf   81
Whole Chicken   49
Whole Wheat Pizza   36
Wholegrain Pitta Chips   11

Y

Your Favourite Breakfast Bacon   14

Z

Zesty Fish Fillets   73
Zingy Brussels Sprouts   40
Zingy Roasted Carrots   43

Printed in Great Britain
by Amazon

38792684R00053